WIRTZ

MATT & TOM OLDFIELD

ULTIMATE FOOTBALL HEROES

WIRTZ

FROM THE PLAYGROUND TO THE PITCH

DINO

First published in the UK in 2026 by Dino Books,
an imprint of Bonnier Books UK,
5th Floor, HYLO, 105 Bunhill Row,
London, EC1Y 8LZ
www.bonnierbooks.co.uk

X @UFHbooks
X @footieheroesbks
www.heroesfootball.com
www.bonnierbooks.co.uk

1 3 5 7 9 10 8 6 4 2

Paperback ISBN: 978 1 78946 930 1
E-book ISBN: 978 1 78946 959 2

The authorised representative in the EEA is
Bonnier Books UK (Ireland) Limited.
Registered office address: Block B, The Crescent Building
Northwood, Santry
Dublin 9, D09 C6X8, Ireland
compliance@bonnierbooks.ie

A CIP catalogue record for this book is available from the British Library

Typeset by Envy Design Ltd
Printed and bound by CPI (UK) Ltd, Croydon CRO 4YY

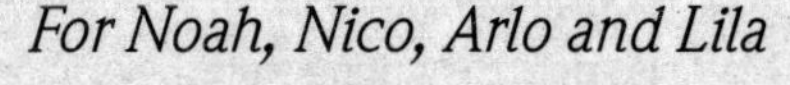

For Noah, Nico, Arlo and Lila

Matt Oldfield is a children's author focusing on the wonderful world of football. His other books include *Unbelievable Football* (winner of the 2020 Children's Sports Book of the Year) and the *Johnny Ball: Football Genius* series. In association with his writing, Matt also delivers writing workshops in schools.

Cover illustration by Dan Leydon.
To learn more about Dan, visit danleydon.com
To purchase his artwork visit etsy.com/shop/footynews
Or just follow him on X @danleydon

TABLE OF CONTENTS

ACKNOWLEDGEMENTS

First of all I'd like to thank everyone at Bonnier Books for supporting me and for running the ever-expanding UFH ship so smoothly. Writing stories for the next generation of football fans is both an honour and a pleasure. Thanks also to my agent, Nick Walters, for helping to keep my dream job going, year after year.

Next up, an extra big cheer for all the teachers, booksellers and librarians who have championed these books, and, of course, for the readers. The success of this series is truly down to you.

Okay, onto friends and family. I wouldn't be writing this series if it wasn't for my brother Tom. I owe him so much and I'm very grateful for his belief in me as an author. I'm also very grateful to the rest of my family, especially Mel, Noah, Nico, and of course Mum and Dad. To my parents, I owe my biggest passions: football and books. They're a real inspiration for everything I do.

CHAPTER 1

LIVERPOOL LIFT-OFF

22 October 2025, Deutsche Bank Park,
Frankfurt, Germany

Florian Wirtz couldn't stop smiling. Maybe it was the thrill of the Champions League. Maybe it was being back in Germany at a stadium he knew well. But something felt different that night as Liverpool were preparing to play Eintracht Frankfurt, and he was buzzing with excitement while he warmed up next to Mo Salah and Virgil van Dijk.

'This is going to be your night, Florian,' Virgil said, giving him a fist bump.

'Are the fans going to cheer you for being a German

player or boo you for playing for Leverkusen?' Mo asked, grinning.

Florian had been wondering the same thing. He was a regular in the Germany squad these days, but the Frankfurt supporters would probably remember that he had played for Leverkusen, another team in the German league. 'My guess is that they'll be booing and whistling at anyone who isn't wearing a Frankfurt shirt tonight!' he replied.

Really, it was the Liverpool fans that Florian was more interested in winning over. His first few months in England had been challenging, especially with a £116 million price tag weighing on him.

He had been such a superstar for Leverkusen that everyone just assumed he would settle in quickly as one of the Premier League's top talents. But it had all been a bigger adjustment than Florian had expected. At times, he didn't look like the same player who had lit up the German league and scored memorable goals at Euro 2024.

In some of his Liverpool games, he had made a run too early and the pass hadn't come. In other games,

he had set off too late and couldn't get to the ball.
The clever touches that had been his trademark for
Leverkusen weren't working either, with his new
teammates on a different wavelength, and it was
impossible not to hear the Liverpool fans groaning.

He wasn't going to give up, though. Like Virgil had
said to him, tonight might be his night, and Florian
just needed a spark to get his Liverpool career up and
running. As more and more fans poured into Deutsche
Bank Park, he went through his last few stretches and
walked back up the tunnel.

When Liverpool manager Arne Slot called for quiet
in the dressing room, everyone turned to look at
him. The team was on a bad run of results, with four
losses in a row, but Coach Slot had kept the practices
fresh and upbeat. They were the Premier League
champions, after all.

'I want to see us get back to being the real
Liverpool,' he told his players as the minutes ticked
down towards kick-off. 'We're not going to feel sorry
for ourselves. Stick together and let's start turning
things around tonight.'

Florian was starting on the right wing, and the formation had a familiar feeling with Jeremie Frimpong, his teammate at Leverkusen and now at Liverpool, behind him at right-back.

'Just like old times!' he told Jeremie as they were leaving the dressing room.

'The dream team!' Jeremie replied, patting him on the back. 'You know I'll be flying forward whenever we get the ball!'

Florian got the usual shiver of nerves when the teams were stepping onto the pitch. The Champions League anthem blasted out of the stadium speakers, and he knew there would be friends and family watching the game closely, as well as German fans and coaches.

In an end-to-end first half, Frankfurt scored first but Liverpool hit back to take a 3–1 lead. Coach Slot still wanted to see more control in the second half, with Florian as a key man.

'Keep getting into those pockets of space,' Coach Slot told him. 'If they're not marking you tightly there, you can pick them apart with your passing.'

When Frankfurt sent more and more players

forward, bigger gaps started to appear. Florian spotted them immediately.

First, he burst free down the right wing, glanced up to see where the strikers were, and then swept in an inch-perfect pass for Hugo Ekitike. 4–1.

'I told you!' Virgil called during their jog back to the halfway line. 'We're getting some Florian Wirtz magic tonight!'

Then Florian touched a simple lay-off to Dominik Szoboszlai, who smashed in a shot from the edge of the box. 5–1. Game over.

This was more like it! With those two assists, Florian felt some of the weight lift off his shoulders, and he proudly joined his teammates at the final whistle when they went over to celebrate with the travelling Liverpool fans.

Florian knew one good game wasn't enough to prove he was a great signing, but it was a step in the right direction.

'I'm just getting started,' he thought to himself, looking up at the Liverpool shirts and scarves in the crowd.

Sometimes, even Florian forgot that he was still only twenty-two. The football world moved at such a dizzying pace that he had to remember to catch his breath when he could. This was one of those moments. Florian grinned and exhaled. Even with some of the challenges so far in his short Liverpool career, he knew how lucky he was to play the game he loved.

CHAPTER 2

TTHE HOME SQUAD

Mornings in the Wirtz house were usually a blur. Little Florian liked to sit at the kitchen table with his big sister Juliane and watch everything going on around them.

They giggled as their dad, Hans-Joachim, rushed past with a slice of toast in his mouth. Their mum, Karin, was laying out bowls of cereal. Then there were hurried footsteps on the stairs. Someone was late for school.

There was a good reason for all the frantic action. Florian and Juliane had eight older stepbrothers and stepsisters, and some mornings it took a miracle to get everyone out of the door on time. But it also created special family bonds.

'We're so lucky,' one of his stepbrothers liked to joke. 'We've got your own five-a-side game anytime we want to play!'

The calendar on the wall was jammed full of after-school activities, and Florian was often along for the ride, whether it was football, handball, swimming or music.

That evening, Karin helped Florian and Juliane put on their shoes in the hallway. It was her turn to do the drop-off and pick-up at football practice, and Florian could see his stepbrother, all dressed for training, waiting impatiently at the door.

Luckily, it wasn't a long drive. After Karin parked across from the practice pitch, she turned to look at Florian and Juliane in the back of the car.

'I'm sorry if this is a bit boring for you,' she explained, wondering how she would keep them entertained during the practice. 'You can bring a ball, but you'll need to stay next to me on the touchline.'

Florian and Juliane nodded, then grinned at each other, and hurried to undo their seatbelts. How could they be bored if they had a football to play with?

Juliane scooped up the ball on the floor in front of her and high-fived Florian. 'Let's go!' she said.

While his mum talked to some of the other parents, Florian found two cones that weren't being used and set them up as goalposts. 'Now we're ready!' he called to his sister.

For the next hour, they were in paradise. They didn't watch a second of the practice because they were too busy with their own game. They took turns shooting, pretending to be professional footballers as they did it. Florian was only four years old, but he could already kick the ball harder than most boys his age.

'Okay, you're goalie now, Flo,' Juliane said, using her brother's nickname and running over to swap with him.

Uh-oh, Florian thought. He slowly walked over and positioned himself between the posts. His sister had such powerful shots. The last few times he had tried to save the ball, his hands had stung for ages.

'You can do this!' Florian told himself. 'Just watch the ball.'

He took a deep breath. Juliane dribbled a little

closer, then stopped the ball. She took a couple of steps back and whacked a shot towards the goal.

Florian felt a flutter of panic but then stuck out his leg and blocked the ball. Yes!!!!!

Juliane couldn't believe it. 'Have you been going to goalie training secretly?!' she asked, laughing.

When Florian got another chance to shoot, he tried to copy the way that Juliane had kicked the ball. He hit his shot hard and low, and it sneaked past Juliane's dive.

Goooooooooooooooooooooooooaaaaaaaaaaaaaaaaaaaa aaaaaaallllllllllllllllllllllllllllll!

Florian jumped in the air and pulled his T-shirt over his head, as he had seen real footballers do.

He pulled it back down just in time to see his mum looking over with her hands on her hips. Florian froze, but then Karin's serious face turned into a smile.

'Nice goal!' she shouted, giving him a thumbs up. 'But we don't all need to see your belly next time!'

Florian and Juliane laughed so much that they fell onto the grass. If this was what football practices were like, they would happily come along any time.

CHAPTER 3

JUST CALL ME "COACH"

'We'll need to have lunch earlier tomorrow,' Hans-Joachim explained as he drove Florian and Juliane to the supermarket. 'We've got to be at football practice by 12:30.'

Florian nodded from the back seat. He was used to the busy weekends by now.

'But then we'll be back later in the afternoon so you can both finish your homework,' Hans-Joachim continued.

Florian sighed. More homework! Then he started thinking about what his dad had just said. It was hard to keep up with all the activities for his stepbrothers and stepsisters, but he couldn't remember ever going to a Saturday football practice at lunchtime.

'I thought training was always on weekdays,' he said. 'Whose practice is it?'

Hans-Joachim allowed a little smile to spread across his face. 'Oh, didn't I mention that?' he said.

Now Florian was confused. 'No!' he said.

'Oh, well it's your first practice for SV Grün-Weiß Brauweiler,' he replied, watching Florian's shocked reaction in the car mirror.

SV Grün-Weiß Brauweiler was a local club, and Florian knew all about the team. Hans-Joachim had been involved for years, and the whole family had spent time there. So Florian would definitely be able to find his way to the pitch! Now he would actually be playing for the club – well, the Under 6 team, at least.

Hans-Joachim was usually involved in the training sessions, with his green tracksuit and a whistle around his neck. But not tonight. He decided to watch from the touchline and give Florian the space to play without giving out the instructions.

Florian expected to feel nervous as he put on his boots, but he was mostly excited. He played football every day – this wouldn't really be any different. He felt like the luckiest six-year-old in the world.

Some of the other boys were laughing and joking while they waited for practice to start, but Florian was happier to be in the background as he got used to this new world. He wasn't quite as shy once the coaches had introduced him to the rest of the team, and he was right at home when the coaches passed out balls for some dribbling drills.

Just like when he played against Juliane, Florian moved the ball quickly and dodged tackles. Just like when he played against his friends, he kept his head up so he could see where his teammates were.

Most of all, he wanted to learn. Two boys had to be reminded to listen when the coaches were talking, but Florian soaked up every word. Even as the coach was still explaining the next exercise, Florian was picturing how he would do it.

At the end of training, the coaches gathered to talk about the session and plan for the next practice. It was also a chance to discuss the players who had stood out. Hans-Joachim walked over to join in.

'Florian looks like a great addition to the team,' one of the coaches said, turning to Hans-Joachim. 'Have you taken him through lots of drills at home?'

'Honestly, it's all pretty natural for him,' Hans-Joachim explained. 'He moves into space without having to think about it – and once he gets the ball under control, no one can take it from him.'

The coaches were always on the lookout for good young players, but skill wasn't the only thing on the checklist.

'You can tell he loves to play and wants to be coached,' another coach pointed out. 'With that kind of attitude, he's going to keep improving.'

Florian skipped back to the car with a big grin on his face. 'That was so fun!' he told his dad. 'Can I come here again?'

Hans-Joachim was grinning, too. 'Well, it looks like we've got another activity to add to the calendar,' he said. 'You're officially part of the team now!'

That became the highlight of Florian's week. He jumped out of bed every Saturday and was dressed in his kit hours before they actually needed to leave.

At training, Florian didn't want the other boys to think of him as the coach's son, in case they thought he hadn't really earned his place in the team. He didn't want any special treatment either.

'Is he still your dad when you're there, or is he the coach?' asked Christoph, a friend who lived on Florian's street, as they walked to school one morning. Christoph always liked to hear the stories from the latest practices.

Florian paused to think about that. 'Well, I try not to call him Dad!' he answered, laughing. 'But "Mr. Wirtz" sounds like we're starting a business meeting!'

That night, Florian put the same question to his dad.

'Just call me "Coach",' Hans-Joachim replied.

The car journeys to practices and games were always chances to talk about football, and Florian liked to ask his dad for advice. If he had a bad game, or he couldn't find a way to improve something, Hans-Joachim was there to give him suggestions.

For instance, during one match later that month, Florian was pushed off the ball again and again, and the referee didn't give him a single free kick.

Florian's frustration boiled over in the car. 'What am I supposed to do?' he asked his dad. 'I was getting to the ball first, and they just shoved me.'

When they got home, a new coaching session began. 'Follow me,' Hans-Joachim said, leading the way through to the living room carpet where Florian and Juliane loved to have their indoor football battles.

'Watch the way I position my body,' Hans-Joachim said, putting his arms out to shield the ball from imaginary tacklers. 'That's the way to match their physicality. Use your arms, your shoulders, your hips. Don't even let them see the ball.'

Florian tried that approach in the next match. Sure enough, defenders couldn't move him as easily, and he even shouldered his marker off the ball once.

'My dad knows what he's talking about!' Florian thought to himself, turning and jogging up the pitch.

CHAPTER FOUR

ACADEMY ACE

Nothing compared to the excitement of playing football. Florian's latest habit was going back onto the pitch after SV Grün-Weiß Brauweiler practices while his dad was talking to the other boys' parents. Sometimes, Hans-Joachim got distracted answering questions, and Florian quietly dribbled the ball around, pretending to twist and turn past defenders and working on new skills.

Florian was soon using those skills to trick real defenders. He wasn't the fastest, but he was unstoppable when he got the ball. While other boys rushed towards wherever the ball was, Florian drifted out to the wings. He also understood that it didn't

help his teammates if he stood still after playing a
pass, so he was always on the move, looking for
a one-two or a through ball.

Hans-Joachim had seen enough youth football
to know the signs: after just a few months of real
football, Florian was ready for the next level. Though
Pulheim was a small town, word travelled quickly
through the football networks, and scouts from some
big German clubs were showing interest.

Academy training would give Florian new targets
to chase, and Hans-Joachim had a feeling that his
son would thrive in a more competitive setting. 'It
would bring out the best in him,' he told Karin. 'I've
seen him play some of his best games against really
good opponents.'

So, if an academy was the next step, what were the
options? Hans-Joachim and Karin talked with some
of the visiting scouts to get a better understanding of
their priorities, and then they spoke to Florian. He was
still so young, but they wanted him to be part of this
important conversation.

Both of his parents knew how the sports world

worked – Hans-Joachim with his experience in football and Karin as a handball player. They wouldn't allow Florian's standards to slip at school, but they wanted him to have every opportunity to pursue his football dreams, too.

In the end, Cologne felt like the perfect choice. It wasn't too far away, and Hans-Joachim knew some of the staff there. The Cologne coaches invited the Wirtz family to visit their academy setup, and Florian was excited to see the main indoor gym, with goalposts marked out on the wall at each end.

Yes, he could picture himself scoring some goals there.

'I like it!' he told his parents. 'How soon can I start playing?'

Karin laughed. 'You'd probably be in that gym now if we'd brought your kit with us!' she said.

'You know me too well!' Florian replied, grinning. 'I should have brought my trainers!'

After signing all the paperwork, it was soon time to join up with the other Cologne academy boys, and the coaches were looking forward to seeing how Florian fitted into their system.

The first session was exhausting, and Florian was dripping with sweat when he hurried over to his water bottle. He hadn't really known what to say at the start when he met so many new faces, but the boys were all soon united by their love of football – and the usual debates began: Lionel Messi or Cristiano Ronaldo? Bayern Munich or Real Madrid?

Eventually, it was time to switch from the drills to a mini-game. In his SV Grün-Weiß Brauweiler matches, Florian had raced all over the pitch, creating chances, taking shots and winning the ball back for his team. He was basically playing three different positions at the same time.

Now he realised he didn't need to do that. The Cologne coaches wanted to explore where Florian could have the biggest impact. In some of the practice games, he was a winger, dribbling and crossing the ball to the strikers. In other sessions, he was the playmaker, dropping a little deeper than the striker and looking for the perfect assist.

There was something magnetic about the way Florian controlled the ball. His touch was good enough to receive passes in tight areas and still wriggle free, and he could hold off bigger players despite being so skinny.

Soon, he was piling up highlights:

A silky stepover that left a defender on the floor.

An outrageous rabona that hit the post.

A long-range volley that flew into the top corner.

After a few weeks, the coaches had reached one main conclusion: Florian was really good wherever he played.

CHAPTER FIVE

SNEAKING MORE TIME AT SCHOOL

Florian put down his knife and fork. He was the first to finish his meal, and he already had plans for what he wanted to do next. It was a sunny Sunday afternoon, and that meant one thing – football.

He was improving every week at the Cologne academy, but it was never enough for Florian. He was always thinking about the next chance to get on the pitch.

'Can I go and play outside with my friends?' he asked.

His parents looked at each other. They had chosen not to have a TV at home so that Florian and their other kids would explore outside instead, so they could hardly say no now. 'Okay, but don't go far and make sure you all stay together,' his mum said eventually.

Florian jumped up from his chair before they could change their minds.

There were lots of other kids in the neighbourhood who loved to play football, so it never took long to find enough boys for a game. Sometimes, they played in the street, making two goals out of jackets. Other times, they set up a pitch at the local park.

It felt like today was going to be a street game, and Florian was just thinking about which street would have the fewest cars when he remembered what one of his stepbrothers had told him:

The school used to be open in the evenings, and we played on the pitch there.

Was that still true? 'There's only one way to find out,' Florian said quietly to himself.

The school was only a few streets away from his house, so Florian decided it still counted as not going 'far', like he had agreed with his parents. He stopped off at his friends' houses, and soon they had a big enough group for a game.

'Where are we going?' Christoph asked as they turned the corner. 'This isn't where we normally play.'

'I need to pick up my homework first,' Florian answered, with a wink.

Christoph was about to reply, but then he realised what Florian was saying. 'The school pitch?' he whispered.

Florian nodded. 'Let's at least see if it's open,' he said. 'The street games are fun, but it's always better when we have real nets and a proper pitch.'

The school field was always in good condition. The grass was cut short, and the white lines around the edge of the pitch were carefully marked.

The excited chatter grew louder and louder as they reached the school. Florian tried to open the gate to the field, but at first it just squeaked back at him. He pulled the handle a little harder, and gasped as the gate inched open.

'Flo, you're a genius!' called Ole, another neighbour who had known Florian for years.

'We've got the whole field to ourselves!' Christoph added. That was a rare treat, because they had to share the pitch with lots of other kids during the school lunch breaks and they were always bumping into other matches.

Today, there was no one in sight, though they all still glanced at the school windows occasionally, expecting to see the headteacher looking back at them.

'Okay, what are we waiting for?' Ole asked. He started making teams and pointing for some of the boys to go down to the other end of the pitch.

'I'm on Flo's team!' Christoph shouted immediately, running over to his friend.

Florian grinned. This was amazing! Their own football pitch. Their little secret.

Ole kicked the ball high into the air, signalling the start of the game. Florian always played well on this pitch – it was probably all the good memories he had there. That day, he curled one shot into the top corner, then volleyed another so hard that the keeper almost flew into the net with the ball. He ran and ran until his legs started to ache.

'My parents always say I need to work harder at school,' Christoph joked. 'Now I can tell them that I'm putting in lots of extra hours here!'

'I don't think these games are going to help you on the maths test next week, though!' Florian shot back.

As the afternoon turned into evening, the boys walked back home. None of them really wanted to leave the field, but they knew this was just the beginning of their secret pitch adventures.

CHAPTER SIX

A WILL TO WIN

From the earliest stages, Florian set himself the challenge of improving every week – at school, or even in his games with his friends. But his training sessions with Cologne were the most competitive, with all the boys sharing the same dream of making it all the way to the first team, and Florian had to be at his best to keep up.

His determination impressed the coaches just as much as his ability on the ball. Like at SV Grün-Weiß Brauweiler, most of the other kids went straight home after practices. They were tired from all the running, but Florian never complained. If anything, he wanted to be even more exhausted.

Extra shooting practice? Yes please.

Dribbling through cones? Sounds great.

Sprints from one end of the gym to the other?
No problem.

Florian was a long, long way from becoming a professional footballer, but it was impossible not to think about that end goal. It was all extra motivation.

Cologne academy games took over the weekends, and Florian was soon travelling from town to town and city to city to play other academy teams. Even though he was still small for his age, the coaches also gave him opportunities to play against older kids. That taught him new lessons – how to make faster decisions and how to outthink bigger defenders.

As he moved through the age groups at Cologne, his teammates became his friends. Naturally, that made their connection even stronger on the pitch. They understood where each other would be, and Florian instinctively knew the runs that the strikers liked to make.

During one warmup session, Florian joked with Charles and Andreas, two of the early Cologne academy boys, as they remembered the highlights from the Under 9s and Under 10s. Now they were preparing for an Under 12s game that night, and it was fun to think about how far they had already come on their journey at Cologne.

The coaches were still giving them the same message, though. The drills were more complicated, and the running was more intense, but the number one goal was to play good passing football.

'Just play your game,' the Under 14s head coach reminded the boys. 'Let's get the ball on the ground and use our skill and speed.'

This Cologne team wasn't built to whack long balls up to a giant striker. They were more technical, just like Florian. Their best game plan was always to pass and move, leaving their opponents tired and dizzy.

Florian was one of the quieter boys in the dressing room. With his calmer personality, he wasn't usually the person telling jokes or rallying the team with loud messages. He preferred to let his play do the talking.

But something changed inside him when he was on the pitch. By now, Florian's friends and teammates all knew the signs. It was almost as if they could see the smoke coming out of his ears. It didn't matter if it was a real game or just a five-a-side kickaround. Florian had to win.

'Come on, we've got time for five more minutes!' he shouted at the end of the latest street football game.

'But we agreed on first-to-five,' Ole said. 'And that goal made it 5–3.'

'Let's do first-to-seven,' Florian pleaded. 'Come on, it's not dark yet.'

'Do you want to explain to my parents why I'm late getting home?' Ole asked.

Florian hesitated. Ole had a point. None of them wanted to get banned from these games.

'Okay, okay,' Florian said, sighing and holding up his hands in surrender. 'But let's play again tomorrow. Same time, same place.'

The football battle might be over for the night, but Florian would still take any chance to compete – board games, races, sit-ups or anything else. Juliane was his usual opponent, but he wasn't short of options in the busy Wirtz house. Though he wouldn't scream or shout, the competitive energy bubbled up inside him, and he was still learning how to channel that into something positive.

Karin and Hans-Joachim sat down with Florian one night after a tough football loss.

'I know what you're going to say,' Florian said, looking at the floor. 'I need to stop taking things so seriously, right?'

His parents smiled. 'Actually, no,' his mum replied. 'We don't want you to change who you are. Part of the reason that you're so good on the pitch is because you really care, and you make others care too. Don't ever lose that.'

'But you've got to take a deep breath sometimes,' his dad added. 'If you're losing, you have to stay cool and find a way back into the game.'

Florian nodded. That made sense. In his next game, he tried to keep those words in mind. This was when the Cologne Under 13s went 1–0 down after a bad mistake by their goalkeeper, but Florian didn't let that affect him. He encouraged his teammates, worked even harder and led the way to a 4–1 win.

That felt good. As he looked over to the touchline where he knew his dad would be standing, Florian saw Hans-Joachim proudly giving him a thumbs up.

CHAPTER SEVEN

A SIMPLE PLAN

When Florian was lining up with other boys from his class, he couldn't stand still. He was so excited to represent his school on the football pitch, and today was the first trial.

Well, for most of the boys, it was a trial. But there was never any question about whether Florian would be picked for the team. He was the best player at the school and could do things with the ball that everyone else could only dream about. But he had been counting the days until he could put on the school's blue-and-white kit. He just hoped that the games would fit into his busy schedule at Cologne.

Coach Roland knew all about Florian's talent. In fact, most of the teachers did. The playground stories had reached the staff room a long time ago.

'You're going to win a lot of games this year, Roland!' they told him.

'Well, after the last two years, I think we're due for some better results!' Coach Roland answered, grinning.

'We'll tell everyone it was your amazing coaching that turned things around,' one of the other teachers joked. 'We don't have to mention that you've got Florian in the team this year!'

But after the first week of practices, Coach Roland saw that it might not be as easy as everyone thought. Florian couldn't play in all eleven positions, and they didn't seem to have many good defenders.

Rather than trying to teach the boys any complicated formations, Coach Roland decided to keep things simple.

'When we don't have the ball, we've all got to work together to win it back,' he explained. 'When we get the ball back, just pass it to Florian.'

The boys all nodded. They knew it was their best chance of winning, and the plan worked. Even if Florian was surrounded by defenders, he could usually escape. Coach Roland had lost count of the number of times that Florian had done that in school practices, weaving in and out to dodge tackles.

The other boys spent most of the games running around. It was tiring work, but no one complained. That was probably because they were piling up wins. Florian scored a hat-trick one week, then four goals in the next game.

But he also understood how to be a good teammate. Any time a teacher or a parent or someone else in their class asked about the latest game, Florian made sure that he mentioned the other players' contributions. Some boys might have been cocky in that situation, but not him. He knew he couldn't win anything on his own.

Florian also wanted to help his teammates develop into better players. That wasn't going to happen overnight, but he showed them some of his Cologne academy drills and patiently practised passing, heading and shooting. It was all about building up their confidence and the overall team spirit.

Coach Roland watched from the far side of the field as Florian played the role of assistant coach and gave out some shooting advice. 'He's even really good at this too!' Coach Roland thought to himself.

But Florian's biggest gift was his special sense for when he needed to take over in games. If his team was under pressure, that was the signal for a solo run or some other trickery to settle everyone down. Then he could focus on linking up with his teammates again.

Every match gave Coach Roland something new to smile about. Florian knew there was less pressure for his school games, and he wasn't shy about trying out new tricks, despite defenders marking him aggressively. That usually meant at least a couple of 'wow' moments where his touch and technique were effortlessly brilliant.

Florian's Cologne coaches helped make it possible for him to play in these school games. They understood how important it was for him, and he worked even harder in his academy sessions to prove that he wouldn't let his standards drop.

'I don't think I could fit any more games or practices into my week,' Florian told Ole one afternoon, scooping up his kit bag ready for practice. 'It's football, football and more football these days!'

'Isn't that the way you like it, though?' Ole asked.

Florian smiled. 'It sure is!' he said.

CHAPTER EIGHT

TALKING TACTICS

Florian's rapid progress at Cologne included more than just his technical ability, and he was taking every opportunity to build on his knowledge of the game. The coaches experimented with a few different formations that year, and Florian was one of the sharpest kids in these moments. He didn't need anything to be explained twice, and he instinctively knew how to adapt and how to quickly spot the opponent's tactics.

The buzz grew as he moved through the Under 13s and Under 14s, leaving a trail of silky passes and memorable goals. He was still one of the smallest players on the pitch, but that didn't stop him from being at the centre of his team's best moves.

As Florian moved into the Under 15s group, his highlights were becoming legendary. Coach Heck, who ran the Cologne Under 17s team, grinned when he heard about the latest moment of genius – a volley from the edge of the box. 'That boy again!' he said to himself.

Later in the week, Coach Heck was sitting in his office. He looked at his watch and decided to walk over to see the last few minutes of the Under 15s practice. He got there just as Florian backheeled a pass effortlessly to a teammate to start an attack.

When the coaches called the players over to the touchline for some final instructions, Coach Heck moved a little closer to listen to the discussion.

One of the coaches looked up and waved. 'We're playing so well that even Coach Heck wants to see the secret formula!' he joked. 'If you boys keep working hard, you might be in his Under 17s squad in a few years.'

Florian looked up. He liked the sound of that.

When another coach explained a new formation

that they would be working on next week, Coach Heck saw a little arm go up with a question.

'If I'm playing on the right and I stay close to the touchline, can the right back make an underlapping run on the inside instead?' Florian asked.

Coach Heck smiled. That wasn't a typical question for a boy of this age. But the coaches didn't look surprised. They just used a little whiteboard and sketched out a few game situations to explain Florian's point to the rest of the boys.

'That was a great question, Florian,' Coach Heck said as they were leaving the practice pitch. 'It's something we're working on with the Under 17s at the moment, and it takes time to get used to playing that way. You should come and join us for one of our video sessions.'

Florian froze. First, he was happy that Coach Heck remembered his name. Second, the idea of spending time with the Under 17s was both amazing and terrifying.

But all this tactics talk was fun for him. It was the way his brain worked. Even before he got the ball, he had a clear picture of the field around him – where his teammates were, and where the defenders were. Once he was dribbling forward, all the options opened up. His coaches sometimes compared him to a chess player, planning three steps ahead and out-thinking the other team.

If I take a few touches inside, the nearest defender will follow me and leave space for one of the strikers to make a run.

If my eyes and body position make it look like I'm going to play a through ball down the middle, all the defenders will tuck in to cover that, and our winger will be unmarked.

It was the game within the game, and he loved it.

Later in the season, Florian was invited to listen to an Under 17s film session, just as Coach Heck had promised. They were reviewing some video clips from their latest match, and Florian sat quietly at the back of the room, soaking up every word. He felt like he was a member of an exclusive club.

The coaches were at the front of the room, pausing the video to point out moments where a player chose the right pass or could have made a better decision. Florian smiled to himself – he could picture the best players in the world doing the exact same sessions at their clubs.

Coach Heck also became a regular spectator at Florian's games. Part of his job was to keep an eye on the young stars in the academy, and there was no doubt in his mind that this little wizard had a big future.

'Florian is already training and playing like a professional,' he excitedly told one of the Cologne bosses. 'There's really no limit to what that kid can do.'

CHAPTER NINE

FLORIAN, THE INTERNATIONAL FOOTBALLER!

'It doesn't get any better than this!' Florian said to himself, looking down at the Germany kit that was folded neatly in front of him.

Over the years, his dad had shown him photos and newspaper stories with older German legends wearing a different version of the country's famous white shirt and black shorts. This time, it was Florian himself who would be wearing the kit.

Scouts had been showing up at Cologne youth team games for weeks, and that included two

German Under 15s scouts. It only took them a few minutes to decide they needed to speak to Florian and his parents.

Those conversations quickly led to a call-up to the next Under 15s squad, and Florian joined other boys from across the country for a few training sessions and a friendly.

'So, have you met Thomas Müller and Toni Kroos yet?' Juliane teased when he video-called home one evening.

'I'm with the Under 15s!' Florian fired back. 'The senior Germany squad isn't exactly hanging out to watch us practise!'

'Oh, I just thought they might have promoted you by now,' Juliane said, shrugging and laughing on the screen.

The first thing that Florian noticed when the Under 15s began training was how good everyone was. He wasn't really surprised. Germany usually had good youth teams. But it was a reminder that even if Florian was the star man in his age group for Cologne, there were lots of other boys across the country with similar skills and similar hopes of becoming professional footballers.

Florian didn't put pressure on himself, though. He could sense that some of the other boys were tense and nervous, and he wondered if that was because of the size of the opportunity or because their parents were pushing them so hard to make the team.

His parents had taken a different approach. Their top priority was for Florian to be happy when he was on the football pitch, so he always played with freedom.

'You're at your best when you've got a smile on your face, so just enjoy it and stay in the moment,' his mum liked to say, and that was great advice for all his new football experiences. Florian didn't look too far ahead, and he didn't let one bad pass or one missed shot affect his confidence.

'He's still small enough that people might think he's younger than fifteen, but the way he plays, it's as if he's actually much older than fifteen,' one of the coaches said, trying to organise his thoughts about Florian.

Right on cue, Florian turned a defender inside out and curled a perfect through ball to set up a goal.

When Florian's name came up in the coaches' meeting room, there were no arguments about whether or not he would be in the starting eleven for the friendly. This was one of the easy decisions. Florian was one of the first names they wrote on the teamsheet.

In some ways, it was a brave choice. Florian was new to the Under 15s squad and some of the other players were such towering figures that it looked like they were in the wrong age group. But Florian made the coaches look like geniuses. He controlled the game in midfield. No one could get near him as he glided around the pitch, always making himself available for a pass and moving the ball from side to side.

The coaches smiled. 'Florian must have played a hundred passes today, and I can't remember him losing the ball once,' one of them said.

Florian finished with three assists, and his teammates voted him Man of the Match. He barely remembered all the names he had tried to memorise over the last few days, but somehow he had built up an instant understanding with the team's strikers.

Taking off his Germany shirt in the dressing room and adding it to the pile on the floor, Florian could still feel the pride running through his body. Just for a second, he allowed himself to imagine that he was playing for the senior team, wearing the same kit and taking on the top teams on the planet.

Florian's Under 15s performance was a step in the right direction, and it was natural to dream about playing for his country in even bigger games, like the European Championships and the World Cup. For now, he would have to settle for watching those matches with his friends – but one day, he wanted to be playing in those tournaments himself.

CHAPTER TEN

THE WONDERSTRIKE

When Florian began training with Coach Heck and the Cologne Under 17s, he knew it was another important milestone. There would be more fans watching on the touchline, more scouts taking notes and bigger defenders trying to stop him.

By now, Florian had found his favourite position. With his quick feet and clever movement off the ball, Florian was a natural attacking midfielder, and the Cologne Under 17 coaches gave him the number 10 shirt.

'You're the playmaker,' Coach Heck said. 'That's what the true number 10s do.'

Florian was ready for it. He knew part of the job

was to be creative and outthink defenders, especially when he got the ball in the spaces between the opposition defence and midfield.

Sometimes, though, he didn't need any help at all to produce jaw-dropping magic.

As the Cologne Under 17s prepared to take the kickoff against Wuppertaler SV, Florian glanced up and spotted the keeper off his line. That wasn't really unusual for the start of the game, when the ball was so far away from the penalty area, but it gave Florian an idea.

He stepped into the centre circle, ready to receive the pass when the referee blew the whistle. The Cologne striker tapped the ball back to Florian, who took one touch to control it and then another to drive a long, looping shot over the heads of the defenders.

The ball seemed to float in the air as everyone turned to watch it. The Wuppertaler SV goalie had spotted the danger a second too late. He scurried backwards but couldn't get a hand to the shot.

Goooooooooooooooooooooooooaaaaaaaaaaaaaaaaaaaaa aaaaaaaalllllllllllllllllllllllllllllll!

There was a stunned silence, then shouts and screams from the Cologne players as they rushed over to celebrate with Florian, who jumped and punched the air. That was a shot he had practised many times in training, so it was no fluke. But he never thought he would use it in a real game.

'I can't believe what I've just seen!' one man said on the touchline, turning to look at his friend. 'That number 10 just put the ball in the top corner from the halfway line!'

Even the referee looked stunned as he got his whistle ready and used it for a second time in the first thirty seconds. Florian later found out that his goal had crossed the line after just 5.05 seconds.

'You could play until you're a hundred and you might never score a better goal!' one of his teammates called out.

Florian laughed. If he was being honest, he knew it was the kind of shot that everyone loved when it went in. But those same people would have waved their arms in frustration if he had sliced it wide.

Coach Heck leaned forward on the touchline to high-five Florian as he ran past.

'Just when I think you can't surprise me with something new, you take a shot like that!' he shouted, smiling.

It was cold and wet enough that day for Florian to put on his gloves, but he was soon sweating as he chased back whenever Cologne lost the ball, following every detail that Coach Heck had covered in the dressing room before the game. He knew his wonderstrike would count for nothing if they lost the game, so he kept battling until the win was secure.

In no time, the video of the goal spread across Germany, and everyone wanted to know about Cologne's little Number 10.

That screamer was one of many special memories that season. The Cologne Under 17s went on to win the national championship, beating Borussia Dortmund 3–2 in the final with some classic Florian moments.

He almost chipped the keeper from forty yards in the first half, and he always seemed to have more time on the ball than anyone else. One brilliant run down the left almost created a goal, but a desperate block deflected the ball.

'Nooooooo!' Florian yelled, falling to his knees in disappointment.

Again and again, he drove forward from midfield. A clever cutback set up another chance, but the Cologne striker fluffed his shot, before Florian weaved through on a solo run but couldn't beat the keeper. He just hoped these misses wouldn't come back to haunt his team.

The last ten minutes felt like an hour, but at last Florian heard the final whistle. He jumped around with his teammates before hugging Coach Heck. All the hard work had paid off, and this Cologne Under 17s team had written itself into the history books.

As Florian grabbed a corner of the silver championship plate and lifted it into the air with his teammates, he just hoped they wouldn't break it.

CHAPTER ELEVEN

AT THE CENTRE OF A STORM

In his academy years at Cologne, Florian had learned lots of new skills – but patience wasn't always one of them.

He was destroying defenders in the Cologne youth teams and doing everything he could to get the first team coaches' attention. Yet the message stayed the same: *your chance will come.*

But when Cologne made further coaching changes, Florian didn't know what to do. There had been so many ins and outs lately. How could he plan for his future at the club if the coaches didn't last more than a season?

That's when Bayer Leverkusen entered the chat. They believed Florian could push them closer to the top of the German league, and they wanted to make a deal.

Before he knew it, Florian was at the centre of a big academy storm – and at first he didn't even understand why. Then he learned about a long-standing arrangement between Cologne, Leverkusen and Borussia Mönchengladbach – the three local clubs had agreed not to swoop in and take players from each other's academies.

For year after year, the deal had stayed in place. Until now.

At Cologne, the anger spiked quickly when news started to spread about Leverkusen's interest in Florian.

'Woah, what are they thinking?' asked one Cologne director. 'Surely they realise we're going to be unhappy about this!'

'We don't swipe academy players from each other,' added another voice. 'It's as simple as that.'

Leverkusen saw it differently. They weren't signing

Florian as an academy prospect. They were signing him to join their first team.

'This is a totally different situation,' a Leverkusen boss insisted. 'We're not talking about a young kid here. Florian is a first team talent and that's how we're going to treat him.'

Did the agreement extend to first team deals? Everyone had an opinion, and Florian was relieved that his parents were representing him in any conversations with the two clubs. He just hoped they could reach an agreement.

'I want to do what's best for my career,' Florian told his mum after the latest round of meetings. 'As long as I feel sure about it, and you and Dad both feel sure about it, then I'm making the right decision.'

Best of all, Florian could see the vision for his future at Leverkusen. There was a firm commitment to get him into German league and cup games to build up his top-level experience, and Hans-Joachim and Karin both liked what they heard from the Leverkusen coaches, who had clearly watched plenty of video clips of Florian's academy games.

Plus, Leverkusen was only slightly further away from Pulheim than Cologne was, so it wasn't as if Florian would be packing up and moving across the country. That was reassuring, because being hours away from his family was a scary thought.

When Florian met with Simon Rolfes, the Leverkusen sporting director, he was determined to make a good impression. But it was still daunting for a sixteen-year-old. He sat down a little nervously and answered questions about his season so far. Then the conversation turned to the future.

'So, Florian, what do you want to achieve in football?' Rolfes asked him.

'I want to be the best player in the world,' Florian replied, with a serious look on his face. As the words came out of his mouth, he was worried that perhaps he was being too honest or setting targets that were too big.

But Rolfes smiled. He loved the confidence, and he could tell that Florian meant what he said. That was the kind of winning mentality that Leverkusen would need if they were going to shake things up in German football.

'Well, we're going to give you the platform and the opportunities to do that at Leverkusen,' he replied. 'We've got a fantastic group of coaches here, and we're focused on challenging the top teams in the country. You're going to be a big part of that.'

Shortly after, Florian was shaking hands and signing a contract with Leverkusen. That meant leaving behind some unhappy faces at Cologne, but all he could really think about was making the most of this amazing chance. There was a very real possibility that first-team action was just around the corner for him.

CHAPTER TWELVE

"SOMETHING SPECIAL"

After all the drama, Florian knew the expectations of him were even higher when he joined the Leverkusen first team, and he wondered what his new teammates would think about all the recent attention.

But there was no reason to worry. The Leverkusen players gave him a warm welcome, and Florian quickly showed why he was being given this chance at such a young age. In his first training session, he scored all five of his shots in the shooting drill, and then he set up three goals in the match at the end of the session.

The whispers began circulating in the dressing room. *'This kid is special!'*

'He's going to be a great player for us.'

'He's a cheat code.'

The coaches understood that this was a project. Florian was going to make mistakes, and he was going to have to adapt to the different physicality in the first team. But that was all part of the learning process. Leverkusen preferred to focus on everything he *could* do, not what he couldn't.

Florian felt his stomach doing backflips when he thought about some of the experienced names in the Leverkusen squad, like goalkeeper Lukas Hradecky, defender Wendell and forward Karim Bellarabi. But it was also reassuring to see a group of younger players there, who had all recently been in the same position that Florian was in now.

'I love it here,' explained Moussa Diaby, a speedy winger, who was twenty-one. 'The coaches really give young players a chance, and the older players are really supportive.'

Leverkusen manager Peter Bosz and his team of coaches met with Florian on the first day to give him a quick introduction on what they expected to see.

They had all kinds of good ideas on how he could take care of his body between games and what types of meals he should be eating.

Day after day, Florian was one of the brightest sparks in training, earning praise from Lukas and Karim, who had both seen lots of young players with this kind of hype come and go in the Leverkusen squad. This situation was different.

The coaches all agreed that it was time to throw Florian into the action. That had always been the plan when he arrived from Cologne, but his obvious talent was making it all happen even faster than expected.

But then the COVID-19 health crisis swept across the world, pausing sports leagues and limiting Florian to indoor workouts. When the games began again, there were no fans in the stadiums. The only way to finish the season was to have strict health processes in place to protect the players, coaches and referees.

Florian was relieved that he had kept up his fitness during the stoppage, because his big chance suddenly arrived, with a first team debut against Werder

Bremen. He excitedly called his family and friends to share the news, then tried to focus on the match.

As the players came out of the tunnel into an empty stadium, Florian blocked out all the thoughts floating through his head. He knew he belonged at this level, and today he would prove it.

It calmed Florian a little to have so many talented teammates around him. Leverkusen had made it a priority to bring in young attackers, and he was part of the front three that afternoon with Moussa and Kai Havertz.

'Let's roll, Flo,' Kai said, while they stood together in the centre circle.

As Florian reached over for a fist bump, he could feel his legs shaking. He looked round to see where the referee was. 'Come on, let's play,' he thought to himself.

It turned out to be the perfect match for Florian to adjust to the top level of German football. Leverkusen cruised to a 4–1 win, and he played his part. Popping up all over the pitch, Florian's Number 27 shirt was a blur of action, and he knew he had done something

right because Coach Bosz also had a role in mind
for Florian in the upcoming match against Bayern
Munich.

'We'll use you as a super sub,' Coach Bosz said,
outlining the plan. 'Whatever the scoreline, we'll get
you on the pitch. It'll be the last thing the Bayern
defenders want to see.'

Florian had made a strong impact so far, but this
was Bayern Munich. THE Bayern Munich. There was
an aura around them any time they played a match.

In many ways, that match was one to forget for
Leverkusen as Bayern powered into a big lead. Florian
watched from the touchline, pacing nervously and
waiting to see when Coach Bosz would give him
the signal.

It came sooner than he expected. Florian was
one of three halftime subs, and suddenly he was
standing next to German league superstars – Robert
Lewandowski, Manuel Neuer, Thomas Müller... the
list went on. These were all players that Florian had
watched and admired since he was a kid.

But that wasn't going to stop him from putting in

tackles and trying to dribble past defenders. As the minutes ticked down, there was time for one more sprint up the pitch as Leverkusen counterattacked. Florian burst into space on the right and called for the ball.

From the right side of the box, he took a touch and saw the full-back racing over. At the last second, Florian faked the shot, cut back onto his left foot and curled a perfectly placed shot past Neuer and into the far corner.

Goooooooooooooooooooooooaaaaaaaaaaaaaaaaaa aaaaaaallllllllllllllllllllllllllllll!

There was no big celebration. His teammates high-fived him, but they all knew there was no way of turning things around that afternoon. It was just a consolation goal, but it meant more than that to Florian. With his head spinning, he just regretted that he had forgotten to grab the match ball at the end of the game as a souvenir.

'It's always something special when you make a debut, especially when you're seventeen,' Coach Bosz said. 'All in all, it was a good performance by him. He wasn't nervous.'

Florian was still disappointed to lose, but the memory of that goal would last a long time. His parents were already starting a collection of articles from the national newspapers and various websites, and he smiled as photo after photo pinged through to his phone.

He was still trying to catch up on all the messages from the last few days. There were texts from his Pulheim friends, including a funny one from Christoph: 'Just remember, we taught you everything you know!'

On that whirlwind afternoon against Bayern Munich, Florian had even set a new record as the youngest ever goalscorer in the German league. At just 17 years and 34 days old, he was becoming the talk of European football.

CHAPTER THIRTEEN

TESTING TIMES

Florian wasn't living the life of a normal seventeen-year-old kid, but he was getting used to that fact. Being a professional footballer was an incredible gift, and he accepted that it also came with some sacrifices. His Friday and Saturday nights were very different from his Pulheim friends' adventures, and that was okay.

He also understood that he had to juggle football and schoolwork. That was part of the deal from the start, and he had promised his parents that he would keep up with his projects and tests. Whether it was late nights writing out notes or study sessions with his tutor, Florian kept his word.

He was getting top marks for his performances on the pitch, too. Leverkusen had been on a good run lately, and Florian was receiving lots of attention as one of the league's breakout stars. That was nice to hear and read, but he knew that he still had plenty to learn before he could even think about being compared to top players around the world.

'Can you even walk through the streets without getting spotted?' Ole had asked when they spoke on the phone.

Florian had to admit that it was getting harder to keep his life private. He liked meeting the fans and smiling for photos, but it was all an adjustment. Luckily, there were experienced players in the Leverkusen squad to ask for advice – and most of the suggestions were helpful, except the idea for a fake moustache and a wig!

The next week, Leverkusen were preparing for a Europa League game against Slavia Prague. But Florian's day was about to take a different path. Coach Bosz called him over at the end of training, and he had a serious look on his face.

'You've been doing a great job, but I've got to leave you out of the squad for this next match,' Coach Bosz explained.

Florian didn't know what to say. He thought about the last few training sessions. He couldn't think of anything he had done that would have upset the coaches. What was this about?

Sensing the confusion, Coach Bosz smiled. 'Don't panic, this isn't some kind of punishment,' he said. 'You've got to be at school this week for your exam.'

Oh, right. The exam. Florian groaned. He had been trying to forget about that. Now it was coming between him and a football match.

'Couldn't you write me a note, Coach?' he asked, with a grin.

'Trust me, an exam is the only thing that could keep you out of the team at the moment,' Coach Bosz said. 'I'm disappointed too, but this is the right thing to do. Your education is really important. Anyways, do you like our chances of convincing your parents that you should skip the exam?!'

Florian laughed. 'You're right,' he said. 'That's never going to happen!'

There was no other option. While most of his teammates enjoyed a relaxing start to the next day before afternoon training, Florian was back in the library. He flipped through books and tested himself on the important information. In some ways, it felt good to have the very normal experience of nervously revising like so many other teenagers.

The hard work paid off. Florian passed the exam, and he was soon back on the pitch doing what he did best. But his teammates couldn't resist cracking a few jokes.

'We missed you, pal!' Moussa said, as they sat down in the club's cafeteria. 'But I'm here anytime if you need someone to check your homework!'

'Yeah, I'm good at maths,' Kai added. 'As long as I've got a calculator, I mean.'

Florian laughed and pretended to throw a napkin across the table. But he didn't mind the banter really. He understood that his school qualifications would give him more options for the years ahead. As his dad often reminded him, a footballer's career was usually over by the time he was in his late thirties. Then what?

That was all a long way off, but Florian knew he was lucky to have so much support from his family, his teachers and his coaches. The best way to repay them was to ace his exams and dominate on the pitch. So far, so good.

Florian signed a new contract at Leverkusen in December 2020, with his parents helping to agree the terms of the deal. That took even more of the pressure off his shoulders. The club had clearly decided that Florian was going to be a big part of their future, and he was feeling more settled every week.

The next task was to climb the table and prove they could compete with the biggest clubs in Germany. Like most young players, there would be more tests ahead, but Florian had the belief that he could overcome anything.

CHAPTER FOURTEEN

BRINGING THE NOISE

The stadiums were still empty as COVID-19 continued to affect people in Germany and around the world. The fans weren't allowed back yet, and Florian really felt their absence for big games like that afternoon's match against Borussia Dortmund.

'We've got to create our own atmosphere today,' Lukas said in the dressing room. 'We want all three points, and Dortmund are a tough team to stop.'

Florian nodded. It was still so strange to play in silent stadiums, where he could hear every word from his teammates and coaches, instead of the fans' nonstop cheers and chants.

But it seemed to suit him just fine. The 2020–21

season was underway, and Coach Bosz was giving Florian the freedom to drift all over the pitch, getting into positions between the midfield and defence that made it difficult for opponents to mark him. From there, he could turn, dribble and make the right pass – all without breaking a sweat.

Would Dortmund be his next victim? The score was locked at 1–1 heading into the final ten minutes, but Florian could sense there would be further chances as both teams chased the win. Another breakaway sent Moussa behind the Dortmund defence, and Florian's eyes lit up.

'I'm with you!' he yelled, sprinting forward and making sure he stayed onside. 'Play it through!'

Moussa waited for more yellow shirts to rush towards him, then slipped a pass across to Florian.

There was green grass in front of him and only the keeper to beat. Florian took a touch to steady himself and rocketed a shot into the net.

Goooooooooooooooooooooooooaaaaaaaaaaaaaaaaaaaa aaaaaaalllllllllllllllllllllllllllllll!

Florian still had enough energy to run over to the

corner flag, forgetting for a second that there were no Leverkusen fans there to join in the celebrations. But his teammates made up for it. Moussa jumped on his back as Florian was buried in hugs.

'Leverkusen made them pay, with a goal from one of the brightest young stars in European football,' the commentator said, reminding everyone that Florian was still just seventeen years old.

Florian never hesitated in those situations. He trusted himself to hit the target, and it didn't matter if it was on his right foot or his left foot. Back in the dressing room, Moussa and Kai appeared with bottles of water, spraying Florian as soon as he came through the doorway.

'That goal deserved to win the game!' Moussa said, hugging Florian. 'You almost ripped a hole in the net!'

A few weeks later, Florian finished off another Leverkusen move in a 5–2 win against Stuttgart. He dribbled forward as defenders backed off, and the ball ended up with Moussa on the left wing. Florian hadn't stopped to admire the move he had started. Instead, he was unmarked in the box as Moussa floated a cross almost in slow motion. It was coming straight to Florian. He watched the ball carefully and directed a header over the keeper and into the net.

Goooooooooooooooooooooooaaaaaaaaaaaaaaaaaaa aaaaaaallllllllllllllllllllllllllllll!

'You're making it look easy!' Moussa told him.

But it only looked easy because of all the effort going on behind the scenes. Leverkusen were doing hours of work to prepare for games, and Florian enjoyed picking up the scouting notes about each opponent. Just as importantly, there was real unity in the dressing room. Egos were parked outside, and they were all cheering each other on.

'My teammates are amazing,' Florian explained when he was asked about his own rise in the game. 'That's the secret, really, and the connection gets even better with every game we play together.'

He had noticed that in the Stuttgart game, where he would turn into space and wouldn't even need to look up to know where his teammates were. He had all their favourite runs and positions memorised in his head, and he believed in himself to get the pass right.

As the season ended, Florian reflected on the goals and assists from his first year at Leverkusen. Some of those big moments had been planned; others were pure instinct. The team finished sixth in the German league, but there was optimism around the club that this was just the beginning of what this squad could achieve together.

Florian felt the same way, and he wanted to come back even stronger next season. With the help of the coaches, he created a list of things to work on over the summer – from gym exercises to heading. If he returned to preseason training as an even more complete player, he knew he could help push Leverkusen to the next level.

CHAPTER FIFTEEN

EURO GLORY WITH THE GERMANY UNDER-21S

If Florian needed a reminder of how quickly he had burst onto the scene, the Under 21s European Championships provided it. The tournament had been divided into two sections. For the first part, in March 2021, Florian was watching on TV at home.

By the time the knockout rounds started in May, he was in the squad. After a couple of training sessions at the team's base in Hungary, he was in the starting eleven. Germany had a really strong team, but Florian was quickly becoming the star of the group, and it was impossible not to notice the extra reporters and cameras that appeared whenever he was the player selected for media interviews.

Florian didn't really have time to stop and think about it all – and he was afraid that if he did, he might wake up and realise it was all a dream.

'How does it feel to be Europe's biggest teenage star?' Juliane joked.

'Oh no, don't start with that!' he replied, laughing. 'I've answered that question a hundred times at this tournament. Luckily, I've got you to keep my feet on the ground!'

There was no joking around when the tournament arrived, though. It was the perfect stage for Florian to announce himself to a bigger audience. After a nail-biting penalty shootout win against Denmark, the Germany Under 21s squad were one win away from the final. Florian had been subbed off by that point, and he could only watch nervously before sprinting onto the pitch to join the celebrations.

That joy just added to the confidence in the dressing room before the semifinal against the Netherlands, one of Germany's rivals. Florian started on the right wing, but the coaches wanted the front three to swap positions regularly. In the first minute, he burst forward, and the Netherlands left-back wasn't sure whether to track the run.

Florian made him pay for that split second of hesitation. Nmecha, another German attacker, curled the ball into the box with the outside of his right foot and landed it in a spot where only Florian could reach it. The keeper had no chance as Florian pounced, poking the ball into the net.

Goooooooooooooooooooooooaaaaaaaaaaaaaaaaaaa aaaaaaalllllllllllllllllllllllllllllll!

The Netherlands players looked stunned. Some of them hadn't even touched the ball yet. But Germany were walking on air, and all the early nerves disappeared in a flash.

Soon, Florian was in the middle of another German counterattack. With defenders backing off, he knew what he wanted to do. He used his teammates as a decoy this time, weaving his way to the edge of the box then creating enough room to fire a low shot.

Florian didn't hit it with full power. He went for

accuracy instead. The ball skidded across the grass and into the bottom corner.

Goooooooooooooooooooooooooaaaaaaaaaaaaaaaaaaaa aaaaaaalllllllllllllllllllllllllllll!

'Are you kidding?!' Nmecha screamed. 'You couldn't hit the target in training yesterday!'

Florian laughed. His teammate was right about that. Florian had scuffed half his attempts wide and ballooned the rest over the bar during the shooting drill at the end of training. Thankfully, he was back on track today.

'I was just saving my goals for when it really mattered!' Florian replied, grinning.

He was still grinning as he jogged back to the halfway line, but there was a long way to go, and the German coaches were pacing on the touchline, barking instructions and reminding the players to concentrate.

Florian felt like he could run through a wall after his goals. He closed down defenders and won more tackles than he could count.

'That's it!' one of the coaches called, clapping. 'Don't give them any time on the ball.'

There was still a nervy finish when the
Netherlands pulled a goal back in the second half,
but Germany held on to reach the final. Florian
was the hero, and everyone wanted to talk to him
about his goals.

What a feeling! He was the match-winner for his
country, just like he had pictured so many years ago,
dribbling around in the park.

But the job wasn't done yet, and Florian was
confident that he had enough energy left for the
final. There was a trophy to win and fans around the
country were counting on him. He could rest when
the tournament was over.

Florian was at the centre of the action in the final
against Portugal. He found space with no one closing
him down, and he saw the chance to give Germany an
early spark. He whipped a quick shot through a cluster
of defenders, but he put his hands on his head as it
deflected onto the bar. Almost!

He was soon leaping and celebrating, though, as
Nmecha scored a goal that none of them would ever
forget. Now they just had to defend.

'Keep going, guys!' Florian called, following his own advice by blocking a cross.

Finally, the referee blew the final whistle and the German players rushed into a big huddle, jumping and cheering. Then they dragged their exhausted bodies up for the trophy presentation. Florian was moving very slowly. His legs ached and he could feel a bruise on his shoulder, but he didn't care.

The next morning, Florian signed every autograph as he left the hotel and walked onto the team bus. He still had the medal in his pocket, and he was already counting the days until he could use this success as a springboard for his next season at Leverkusen.

CHAPTER SIXTEEN

HISTORY-MAKER

When his football life was going well, Florian tried
to enjoy the ride. But he also knew that there were
dangers in getting too absorbed in all the social media
clips and glowing match reports.

There were so many famous examples of teenagers
who were billed as 'the next big superstar' but, for
various reasons, never fulfilled their potential. Some
of them were already off the radar. So Florian wasn't
going to take anything for granted, especially when
he had lots of milestones to hit before he was even a
proven first-team player.

He was very happy with a quiet life off the field.
His practices and matches brought more than enough

excitement, as did any Wirtz family meet-up, and he wanted to keep his focus on his football as much as possible.

When he had signed a new contract at Leverkusen on his eighteenth birthday, Florian couldn't think of a better possible present, and the 2021–22 season was off to a flying start, with Coach Gerardo Seoane now in charge.

Florian scored the final goal in a 4–1 win over FC Augsburg, and suddenly he couldn't miss. He was on the scoresheet in a loss to Dortmund, and he fired in the winner in a comeback victory in the Europa League.

'Someone's been putting in extra work!' Moussa said. 'You're a goal machine this year!'

Florian laughed. The hours and hours of shooting practice had been worth it.

Every week, it seemed like Florian was setting a new record as the youngest player to achieve something.

The youngest player to score 5 goals in the German league.

The youngest player to score 10 goals in the German league.

The youngest player to play 50 games in the German league.

'This guy seems to make history every time he steps onto the pitch,' Lukas told reporters, putting his arm around Florian as he walked past.

There was even more reason for Florian to smile when he was called up to the Germany senior team for the latest World Cup qualifiers. Coach Joachim had already named him in an earlier squad, but this time Florian was expected to play. He made his international debut as a substitute against Liechtenstein, and he didn't let his shirt out of his sight after the game. He wanted that for his collection.

Coach Joachim shook Florian's hand when he saw him in the dressing room. 'Well done tonight,' he said. 'Everyone told me I'd enjoy working with you, and they were right! You've got a bright future ahead of you, Florian.'

Back at Leverkusen, instead of hoping to score, Florian was going into games *expecting* to score.

His teammates were looking to him even more to be the match-winner, and he loved that responsibility.

At home to Mainz, Leverkusen were struggling to break through a tight defence. They had a goal disallowed, Moussa had a shot saved and the fans were getting nervous.

'It's time!' Florian thought to himself. They needed a moment of magic, and he was the man to provide it.

When Jeremie Frimpong, Leverkusen's speedy right-back, burst forward on the right, Florian got into position for a pass.

'Give and go!' he shouted, using his eyes to show where he wanted Jeremie to run.

Jeremie got the message. He laid the ball off and kept running as Florian played the one-two pass to him. It looked like Jeremie was going to whip a cross right in front of the keeper, but he changed his mind at the last minute.

Florian was unmarked for a cutback, and Jeremie heard his shout just in time. There was still work to do as the ball bounced at Florian's feet, but he shifted it slightly and swept a low shot past the goalkeeper.

Goooooooooooooooooooooooooooaaaaaaaaaaaaaaaaaaaa aaaaaaalllllllllllllllllllllllllllllllll!

'There was only one place that ball was going!' Jeremie shouted, running over to Florian. The fans were back at BayArena, Leverkusen's home ground, and the noise was deafening.

Leverkusen were playing the kind of football that made everyone want to watch their matches, and there weren't going to be many 0–0 draws when Coach Seoane was sending his team out to entertain.

But Bayern Munich set the standard in the German league, winning title after title. They were the team to beat, and they seemed to get stronger every year. If Leverkusen were going to close the gap, they had to learn how to match Bayern.

Florian was excited to test himself against the champions in their upcoming game, but it turned out to be one of the most miserable days of his football career. Bayern scored five times in the first half, leaving Leverkusen stunned.

It was a very quiet dressing room that day, but the mood was different by the time Florian arrived for the next training session. Leverkusen had made a lot of progress over the last year, but maybe the embarrassment of losing like that in front of their own fans to Bayern was the pain that would drive this squad to get even better.

'That's the level we're trying to get to,' Florian told his parents. 'We've seen it up close, and now we're even more focused. You could feel it at practice. We all believe we can be as good as Bayern.'

Now they just had to prove it.

CHAPTER SEVENTEEN
ACL AGONY

Florian was one of Leverkusen's biggest danger men now, and defences hadn't worked out how to stop him. Sometimes, he was on the right. Other times, he drifted out to the left. But wherever he was, he created scoring chances.

He had been looking forward to facing Cologne that weekend. He had great memories of his time there, and he saw lots of friendly faces in the stadium that day. But then disaster struck.

When the ball bounced to Florian at the edge of the box, he knocked it past one tackler with a quick touch. As he stretched to reach it, his legs got tangled with another Cologne defender, and he felt a sharp pain in his left knee as he tumbled to the ground.

'Argh!!' he screamed, whacking the grass with his hand.

The Leverkusen physios rushed over and tried to calm him down.

'Something snapped in my knee!' Florian called out, staying curled up on the ground. He was afraid to move and make things even worse.

'Okay, we're here with you,' one of the physios explained, while the other signalled for a stretcher. 'Just take a deep breath.'

But it was hard to think about anything other than the injury. How serious was it? Would he miss many games?

Back in the dressing room, Florian sat on the treatment bench while the physios took a closer look at the injury. They gently tested his knee and he winced in pain.

There would be more tests and more visits from doctors – and then came a clear answer. Florian had torn the ACL ligament in his knee. He fought back tears as he digested the crushing news.

He had heard enough about ACLs to know
that this was one of the worst injuries for any
footballer. His heart sank as the doctors detailed
the surgery he would need and the typical recovery
period. His head was spinning with all the details,
but luckily his parents were there to ask the
right questions.

The one thing that Florian knew for sure was that
his season was over.

The doubts crowded into his head. 'What if it heals
well but I'm never the same player again?' he asked
his mum one evening.

'I know this is tough to hear, but you just have to
take it one day at a time,' Karin replied, sitting down
next to Florian. 'Remember what the doctors said. If
you follow all the steps and all the exercises, you'll
give yourself a great chance.'

Florian nodded. He had been reading about ACL
injuries. In the past, it was a career-ending injury.
But now athletes were recovering in roughly a year
and returning to play at a high level again. Those were
the positive thoughts he needed to focus on.

'This is just the latest hurdle for me to overcome,' he told Juliane when she visited him after the surgery.

'We're all going to be there to help with the rehab,' she said, smiling. 'You've got a whole team of Wirtz personal trainers ready to order you around!'

'Yeah, I bet you can't wait for that,' Florian answered, laughing. It was going to be a long road back to full fitness, but it made a huge difference to have his family by his side.

Slowly, he made progress, checking off each target. He went from the hospital bed to crutches, then to walking and exercising. When the Leverkusen doctors agreed that he could start doing more work in the gym, Florian set his alarm for 5 a.m. and went on the treadmill and other gym machines for as long as they would let him. It wasn't a real football practice, but it felt closer to what his teammates were doing.

He saw Lukas, Jeremie and Moussa whenever he was at the training ground, and that was a boost, too. In fact, the whole Leverkusen dressing room encouraged Florian to keep going with his comeback.

'We miss you, man!' Jeremie said. 'We need you back, but we want you to be a hundred per cent ready.'

As Florian reached the final stages of his recovery, he accepted that this was all part of his football journey. It probably wouldn't be the last obstacle he had to face, but this long rehab process had reminded him to never take his football career for granted.

CHAPTER EIGHTEEN

A PROUD BROTHER

From an early age, it had been clear that the football brilliance in the Wirtz family didn't end with Florian. His dad and stepbrothers were good players, and Juliane had been a tough opponent in their childhood games. Now Juliane's own football career was taking off in the German women's league.

Like Florian, she had made her breakthrough at Cologne before moving to Leverkusen, and she was developing into a talented midfielder.

Florian's injury and recovery had kept him away from the pitch, but it couldn't stop him from being in the stands to see his sister play. Whenever he saw Juliane charging around and winning tackles, it brought back great memories of all their childhood battles.

'The last two matches have been our best performances of the season,' she told Florian on the phone. 'We can make it three wins in a row on Saturday.'

'Well, I'll be able to see that for myself,' Florian said, a little mysteriously.

Juliane smiled. 'You're coming to the game?' she asked excitedly.

'I'll be there!' Florian said. 'So I'm expecting at least two goals!'

It was a great distraction, too. Florian had been thrilled to see his own Leverkusen team surging towards a third-placed finish in the German league, but it really hurt to miss out on important games at the end of the season. As Florian walked carefully up the steps at Juliane's game, he got chills at being so close to the action again. There was the smell of the freshly cut grass and all the balls on the pitch for the warmup drills.

Photographers had spotted Florian at some of

Juliane's games earlier in the season, but he knew how to avoid them now. He didn't want to take any of the spotlight away from his sister. He was just happy to watch from the stands, and that had become a lot easier without his crutches.

'It feels like only yesterday that we were playing football on our family camping trips,' Juliane told him when he saw her in the tunnel before the game. 'We always had a ball in the car, no matter where we were going!'

Florian laughed. 'Yeah, we never missed a chance to play, even if it was only for ten minutes,' he said.

'So, any last-minute advice for today's match?' she asked.

'Just be yourself,' Florian said, then he smiled. 'Oh, and make sure you don't foul anyone like that time when you tripped me in the living room and I broke a plate.'

Juliane laughed. 'I wish I had the video of that,' she said. 'Partly because I'm sure I got the ball, and partly just to see your face!'

As Florian sat down next to his parents, he was

surprised to feel a little nervous. He really wanted
Juliane to play well, and it was nice to feel some of
the pre-match jitters for the first time in months.

But most of all, he was so proud of his sister.
Juliane had always loved football as much as he had,
and she had never given up on her dream of playing
professionally, even when there weren't as many
opportunities in women's teams in Germany.

That afternoon, Juliane was unstoppable. She was
everywhere, winning tackles in one penalty area, and
then sprinting to the other end of the pitch to support
attacks. She fired one shot slightly wide and another
clipped the post. But Juliane wouldn't be denied. In
the second half, it was her first-time pass that set up
the Leverkusen winner.

In the crowd, Florian was standing and cheering.
It was a pass he would have been proud of, too.

CHAPTER NINETEEN

LEARNING THE XABI PLAYBOOK

When the 2022–23 season kicked off, Florian was still going through his daily exercises. He had moved on to some light jogging to build up his stamina, and the Leverkusen physios were finally happy for him to start doing shooting and dribbling drills.

It felt good to unleash some of the frustration, even when he was shooting at an empty net. The next test would be doing all the same things – passing, dribbling, shooting, running, jumping – with the intensity and physicality of a real game. It wasn't enough just to be able to run. He needed to get back to peak levels, ready for the Bundesliga and international games with Germany.

He could only watch as Leverkusen made a slow start to the season, winning just one of their first eight league games. With the panic building, Coach Seoane was sacked, and that left even more questions for the club to handle.

The main solution to those questions came via Seoane's replacement, Xabi Alonso, who didn't have much managerial experience but had shown his intelligence during his playing days. Florian knew all about Xabi's great career with Liverpool, Real Madrid and Spain. He was a genius on the ball, and Florian hoped Xabi would want Leverkusen to play with that same stylish swagger. But the priority was to climb away from the relegation zone, and the team was soon picking up points again.

One advantage of the club's cautious approach to bringing Florian back into the starting lineup was that he had time to analyse what his new manager wanted to see from his players. As Florian began to join in with portions of training sessions, he stood on the side next to Xabi and learned more about his game plan and his football philosophy. Florian immediately noticed that he and Xabi thought about football the same way – they were clever players who saw the game a few seconds faster than their opponents.

Florian was back on the pitch in January 2022 to join in the battle, and he wanted to know everything he had missed over the past few months. Some days, he needed a reminder that his body was still catching up, and the coaches were quick to step in and tell him to take a breather. He couldn't just press a button and return to his pre-injury form.

As Leverkusen found more of an identity, Florian was going to be a key man in Xabi's system, and he liked the team that was taking shape around him. His manager wasn't shy about giving him praise either.

'There are good players and there are players who look good on the pitch,' Xabi told reporters. 'The player who looks good does things that are nice, but not necessarily efficient. Why is Messi so good? Because he knows how and when to play simple passes. Messi says: "You're in a better position? Here, there you have the ball!" It's not always about making the most brilliant move, but the best and smartest. Florian can do that. That's why he's so good.'

When Florian heard those comments, he grinned. He had a manager who understood his game, what made him special and how to get the best out of him. That was rare.

Florian would never be the loudest player on the pitch, but he could still be a leader. He was showing that on the pitch, setting an example with his consistent performances and pulling Leverkusen up the league table. With win after win, they were closing in on the top six. Their brilliant form even included a 2–1 victory over Bayern Munich.

When Florian and his teammates travelled to face Schalke, they knew that a few more wins would secure a place in next season's Europa League. Jeremie put Leverkusen ahead, then Florian played a slick one-two to create a chance in the box. He dribbled on, kept his cool and poked a shot past the keeper.

Goooooooooooooooooooooooooaaaaaaaaaaaaaaaaaaaa aaaaaaalllllllllllllllllllllllllllll!

Now he was really back!

'Let's goooooooo!' he shouted.

'Classic Flo!' Jeremie called.

When the season ended, Leverkusen had clinched sixth place and excitement was sweeping around the club ahead of the next season. Xabi gathered his players for a few final comments, reminding them to enjoy the summer and be ready to chase bigger targets when the league kicked off again.

Florian was already building a plan for that. As he thought about the past two seasons, he knew there were opportunities to have a bigger impact on games. It was nice to have good touches or sharp passes. It was helpful to give the team nonstop running. But it was the goals and assists that really mattered. That's what would decide wins and losses.

Most of all, that's what would decide who lifted the trophies – and Florian was ready to deliver.

CHAPTER TWENTY

A SEASON OF SURPRISES

From the first game of the season in the German Cup, Leverkusen settled into a great rhythm. They were dynamic, fast and creative, and Florian was loving it.

As he looked around the dressing room, he saw a team that was confident, hungry and ready for a good season. How good? He wasn't sure. But their games were definitely going to be exciting. Leverkusen had Jeremie flying up and down the right wing, and Alejandro Grimaldo doing the same thing on the left wing. Granit Xhaka was the midfield engine, and Victor Boniface gave them pace and power up front. Florian's job was to link all of that talent together.

After plenty of time to assess his squad, Xabi had a clear plan for how he wanted the team to play.

'Don't think about who the opponent is, or the score,' he explained. 'We can make a big statement with the way we play early in the season, and that starts today.'

Leverkusen showed no mercy, and Florian scored one of the goals in an 8–0 win. It was the first sign that this year would be different, and the rest of the league was about to find out the hard way.

'This is the way we want to play,' Xabi explained. 'Good football, exciting and unselfish. When we do all those things, we're a great team.'

More and more of the Leverkusen attacks were flowing through Florian. He was calling the shots like the conductor of an orchestra, and the fans spent every game on the edge of their seats, waiting for the next highlight.

With his team hanging onto a 2–1 lead against RB Leipzig, he saw Jeremie break free on the right wing. Florian and Jeremie had been teammates for long enough to know how to create chances from these kinds of positions. Florian ran forward but stopped just inside the box, and Jeremie's cutback arrived in the perfect spot.

Before the defenders could react, Florian swept a low shot into the bottom corner.

Goooooooooooooooooooooooaaaaaaaaaaaaaaaaaaa aaaaaaalllllllllllllllllllllllllllll!

After that goalscoring start, Florian was flying, and he had an even more spectacular moment against Freiburg a couple of months later.

Jeremie slid a pass down the line, and Florian chased it with a Freiburg defender following him. He slowed down as if he was just going to shield the ball. Then, just as the defender relaxed, Florian spun to his right at lightning speed, escaping and dribbling into the box.

His marker tried to recover, lunging for a block, but Florian tricked him again. Instead of shooting or crossing with his right foot, he turned onto his left foot, keeping the ball close to his body. Other stunned defenders appeared – just not fast enough. Florian danced a few steps further to get a better angle, then whipped a shot into the net.

*Gooooooooooooooooooooooooaaaaaaaaaaaaaaaaaaa
aaaaaaalllllllllllllllllllllllllllllll!*

'Whoa!!!!!' Jeremie screamed, jumping on Florian's back. 'That was cold, man! The defender is still picking himself up off the floor!'

Florian grinned. He couldn't wait to see the replay. It was surely a contender for goal of the season!

Even with Leverkusen's hot start, everyone was still picking Bayern Munich to win the league, and Florian couldn't really blame them. Bayern had been champions for eleven seasons in a row, and now they even had Harry Kane as their top striker.

But maybe that just meant it was time for a change at the top. Leverkusen were clicking and suddenly they had eleven wins and a draw from their first twelve league games. There were still some doubters, but Florian and his teammates knew the truth. They were real title contenders.

There was one obvious way to convince the skeptics: keep winning.

'At the start of the season, there are usually a few teams that fly up the table, but then they fall back,'

Florian reminded his parents at the latest family meal. 'We don't want that to happen to us, so we can't afford to relax.'

Part of the Leverkusen secret seemed to be the togetherness within the squad. It really felt like one big family, and Florian looked forward to the bus journeys and flights with his teammates. The music was usually pumping, and they all loved swapping football stories. Of course, winning always helped!

The dressing room was bubbling with confidence, and it got louder and louder with every victory.

3–0 against Eintracht Frankfurt, with Florian scoring the third.

4–0 against Bochum, with Florian involved in two of the goals.

And 3–0 against Bayern Munich – a result that sent shock waves around the country.

With Leverkusen charging ahead at the top of the table, the conversation changed across the country. It wasn't a question of whether they could win the title anymore. It was whether they could win the Treble!

Florian didn't want to get distracted by that

possibility, but Leverkusen were still crushing teams in the German league and cup, as well as the Europa League. No one seemed to be able to keep up with their speed and movement.

'One game at a time,' Xabi reminded his players as they went through another detailed training session. 'There's still a long way to go.'

Florian knew his manager was right, but it certainly felt like Leverkusen were in the middle of an unforgettable season.

CHAPTER TWENTY-ONE

SEVEN SECONDS

When Florian wasn't tearing through defences for Leverkusen, he was busy becoming a key part of the German national team. Julian Nagelsmann had taken over from Coach Joachim, and he was building a new squad for the big tournaments ahead. Florian had missed the 2022 World Cup because he had been recovering from his knee injury, but Euro 2024 was fast approaching. There was no way he was missing that.

During this latest international break, Germany were playing a friendly against a France team packed with big-name stars like Kylian Mbappé and Ousmane Dembélé. But they had their own talent too. Florian had spent the last few days learning from Toni Kroos and Joshua Kimmich, and every training session was a chance to build chemistry with the rest of the squad. That wasn't easy to do when they only saw each other for a few days during each international break, but the veterans had done a great job of welcoming the younger players.

It was especially important because this German team was in a transition phase. Florian and Jamal Musiala were emerging as the shining stars of the future, and it was only a matter of time before they were leading the next generation.

This match was coming at a great moment for Florian, who was playing the best football of his life. He was excited to bring his Leverkusen form into an international game, and it felt like a good sign that Coach Nagelsmann had picked him in the starting lineup.

'Don't give them a chance to settle,' Coach Nagelsmann said, pacing around the dressing room and looking at his players. 'Even though it's a friendly, the crowd is going to be loud. We need to strike first and put them under pressure. Start fast, guys.'

Germany would be kicking off, and Toni signalled

to Florian, who gave him a thumbs up. Message received. Translation: it was time to try something they had been working on in training.

When the kick-off went back to Toni, he swivelled in the centre circle and surprised France by clipping a pass forward to Florian, who controlled it instantly with his left foot. Two French defenders hesitated, and that gave him time to dribble forward. He took a second touch, then a third. Still no one closed him down. Now he was almost insulted.

Florian looked up and saw he was twenty-five yards out. 'Why not?' he thought.

He took aim and fired a powerful shot that skimmed off a defender's back and flew into the top corner. The keeper didn't even move.

Goooooooooooooooooooooooooaaaaaaaaaaaaaaaaaaa aaaaaaalllllllllllllllllllllllllllll!

Florian slid on his knees near the touchline – he could hardly believe it. His first goal for the senior Germany team! Some fans were still coming into the stadium and looking for their seats, and it was already 1–0.

'At least someone was listening to me!' Coach Nagelsmann joked. 'That definitely counts as starting fast!'

Jogging back to the centre circle, Florian could see the France players were stunned. Mbappé was just staring blankly, like that goal had been a bad dream or a ghost. 'Even Kylian would have been proud of that one,' Florian thought to himself.

It was only after the game that he got the official timing for the goal. *Florian had scored after just seven seconds!* It was Germany's fastest ever international goal.

The rest of the match was a tighter battle, but everyone wanted to talk about Germany's lightning start and whether that move had been part of the game plan.

'I can't give away all our secrets, can I?' Florian joked. 'But that was a routine we practised a lot this week.'

Even in his short career, he had been part of hundreds of free kick and corner routines, and that was becoming a bigger part of the preparation for teams. No matter how long Florian and his teammates practised them, there were no guarantees that they would work in a game. But this time, Germany had done it perfectly and caught France half-asleep.

While he was packing his bags to return to Leverkusen, Florian couldn't help but think about Euro 2024. He hoped he had impressed Coach Nagelsmann with his work rate and the quality of his playing – and surely his goal had increased his chances of being involved in that tournament.

With this moment of genius coming in the middle of an amazing season with Leverkusen, it felt like Florian could do nothing wrong. He wasn't sure he believed that himself, but he hoped there were plenty more goals and assists left in this run.

CHAPTER TWENTY-TWO

UNBEATABLE

Back at Leverkusen, the buzz kept growing. Sometimes the first training session after an international break could feel like a gentle stroll, but this time it was different. Everyone was focused. Everyone was hungry to get back on the pitch.

It wasn't always pretty, but Leverkusen stretched their unbeaten run at the top. With a few league games to go, they still hadn't lost a single game. If anything, they were becoming stronger and stronger.

'We can't afford to get sloppy now,' Xabi explained. 'We've worked too hard to get to this point.'

Florian and his teammates weren't about to give up their unbeaten league record without a fight. They battled to the end of each game, finding dramatic late goals, just when it seemed like they had lost.

'We're not Leverkusen any more, we're Neverlusen!' Florian told Juliane. 'Get it? Never losing!'

It would have been so easy to just accept that a loss was going to happen at some stage. But that's not what the great teams did, and Florian knew it.

'This is our time,' Jeremie told Florian, glancing over to see the fourth official holding up the electronic board and showing eight minutes of added time. Two minutes later, Leverkusen equalised.

'As long as there's time left on the clock, we're still alive!' Florian shouted, running to join the pile of players behind the net. 'We don't quit!'

There had been so many different heroes during the season. But in the biggest moments of the biggest games, Leverkusen looked to Florian. When they travelled to Italy to play Roma in the Europa League, the home fans booed and whistled to make the stadium as hostile as possible for Florian and his teammates.

That atmosphere might have shaken some teams, but it had the opposite effect that night on Leverkusen. Florian felt the adrenaline running through his body, and he could tell that the whole dressing room was fired up.

In the first half, a bad back-pass gifted Grimaldo a clear path to the net, but the angle was tight. Luckily, Florian was racing forward to make life easier for him. Grimaldo squared the ball to him, and Florian did the rest, placing a shot into the bottom corner.

Goooooooooooooooooooooooooaaaaaaaaaaaaaaaaaaa aaaaaaalllllllllllllllllllllllllllll!

'You're the man!' Granit yelled, wrapping Florian in a big hug.

The run kept going. When Florian arrived at BayArena for a match against Werder Bremen, all he could think about was clinching the title. Leverkusen were one win away.

'This is it!' Florian told Jeremie as they changed for the warm-up. 'This is the day we can become Leverkusen legends for life.'

Grimaldo appeared next to them. 'I couldn't sleep

last night,' he said. 'Every time I closed my eyes, I started thinking about what it would be like to lift the trophy.'

Florian had never heard the BayArena crowd to sound so loud – and the game hadn't even started. The volume went up another level as Victor and Granit settled the nerves to give Leverkusen a 2–0 lead, before Florian took over to add a few more highlights to his collection.

In the second half, he turned with the ball twenty-five yards out, and there was only one thought in his mind. Before anyone could close him down, he thumped a swerving, dipping shot that rocketed into the net.

Goooooooooooooooooooooooooaaaaaaaaaaaaaaaaaaaa aaaaaalllllllllllllllllllllllllllll!

'Now it's a party!' Florian said, waving to the fans behind the net.

But he wasn't done yet. A long pass looped over the Werder Bremen defence, and Florian was in the clear. He glanced over to check that there was no offside flag. There were no defenders in sight, and he calmly tucked his shot past the keeper.

*Goooooooooooooooooooooooooaaaaaaaaaaaaaaaaaaa
aaaaaaalllllllllllllllllllllllllllllll!*

Florian looked up into the stands and saw everyone singing. There were flags and banners everywhere. The Leverkusen fans were in dreamland. Red flares lit up the sky, with smoke spreading around the pitch.

Now there was no reason to keep running really. The game was won. The title was coming to Leverkusen. But Florian wanted a hat-trick. He got himself into space and could hardly believe his eyes when he got the ball in the box again. The fans were already standing as he drove a low shot into the bottom corner.

*Goooooooooooooooooooooooooaaaaaaaaaaaaaaaaaaa
aaaaaaalllllllllllllllllllllllllllllll!*

'Incredible!' Xabi said. It was the perfect word to sum up Florian, the hat-trick and this whole season. He finished the season with eleven goals and eleven assists in the German league.

At the final whistle, the joyful home fans sprinted onto the pitch. Florian was celebrating with Jeremie and Granit, and he just had time to high-five some supporters before making it safely to the dressing room. Soon they were all singing and dancing as they counted the minutes until the trophy ceremony.

Leverkusen had to settle for a league and cup double in the end. After fifty-one games without a loss that season, they finally stumbled in the Europa League final, losing 3–0 to Atalanta. Florian had almost forgotten what it felt like to walk off the pitch after a loss. This one stung, but nothing could deflate the mood in Leverkusen after such a dream year. The players were heroes across the city, and Florian knew this bond would last a lifetime.

CHAPTER TWENTY-THREE

GERMANY'S GOLDEN BOY

Florian was shaking with excitement when he joined his teammates for Euro 2024. It was a once-in-a-lifetime chance to play in a major tournament *for* Germany, *in* Germany, and his phone was buzzing nonstop with messages from friends and family. He had run out of ideas on ways to get tickets for all the people who had asked.

Lots of people were talking about Spain, England and France as the tournament favourites, but Florian knew the German squad could compete with anyone.

'We have to get through the group stage before we can start thinking about playing any of those teams,'

Florian told Juliane. 'But you can feel the confidence in the squad. We believe we can go all the way.'

The nerves were building in the warm-up, and Florian watched as the stadium went from near-empty, to half-full, to jam-packed. He smiled and waved to a group of fans standing near the tunnel.

'Score a goal for us, Florian!' one boy shouted, wearing a Wirtz 17 shirt.

'You're my hero!' a little girl called.

This was what made it so special to be playing this tournament at home, with so many German fans sharing in the experience.

'We're the tournament hosts, we're playing the first match, and this is our chance to set the tone,' Coach Nagelsmann told his players, his voice growing louder and louder in the dressing room.

Once the pre-game show was over, it was time for Germany to get down to business. Everyone was expecting them to win this first game against Scotland, but the coaches' message all week had been about staying focused.

In the first minute, Florian caught the Scotland

defence half asleep. Antonio's long pass floated down the middle, and Florian was the quickest to react. He sprinted to catch up with the ball and poked a quick shot, but the keeper blocked it as he raced off his line.

Florian grinned. This was going to be a fun ninety minutes if Scotland defended like that!

Ten minutes later, Florian made his latest run into the box. This time, Toni had fired the ball out to the right wing, and Joshua Kimmich dribbled inside before spotting Florian, who was waving his arms to get his teammate's attention.

Joshua's pass was perfect and right into Florian's path. He whipped a first-time shot across the keeper, who could only tip it onto the post and watch as the ball rolled into the net.

Goooooooooooooooooooooooooaaaaaaaaaaaaaaaaaaa aaaaaaalllllllllllllllllllllllllllll!

What a feeling! Florian ran over to the corner flag to celebrate, but that section of the crowd was full of sad Scotland fans. Before he could turn around and find all the German supporters, he was smothered in hugs and high-fives.

'The Wirtz wizard does it again!' Toni called.

Florian could see the German flags waving wildly in the crowd, and it felt amazing that he had played a part in their joy. Now the fans were urging their team forward again and again. Jamal and Kai scored to make it 3–0 at half-time, and Scotland were down to ten men.

Coach Nagelsmann used the big lead to rest some of his starters, and Florian soaked up the applause from the home fans when he was subbed off. Germany went on to win 5–1, and suddenly everyone was paying attention to this exciting young team.

'It's about time!' Florian said, laughing.

Germany topped the group, and Florian loved seeing Euro 2024 fever sweeping across the country. Sometimes, it was difficult not to daydream about what it would be like if they won the tournament, but Florian had played enough football to know the dangers of looking too far ahead.

After all the group stage excitement, Florian was disappointed to start on the bench against Denmark in the second round, but Coach Nagelsmann reassured him that he was still going to be involved in the action.

'You'll have a part to play for us,' he explained. 'Stay ready.'

Florian had the same role for the quarterfinal against Spain, but there was no sulking. He had always been a team player and that wasn't going to change. But when Germany fell behind 1–0, they needed a moment of magic – and Coach Nagelsmann turned to Florian.

'We just need one chance,' Florian mumbled to himself, waiting for the Spain keeper to kick the ball.

The clock ticked on to 86 minutes, 87, 88. It was now or never.

Just then, Florian pounced on a loose ball at the edge of the box and knocked it back to Toni, who sprayed a pass out to the left wing. Florian joined the crowd of players rushing into the box as the cross came in.

His heart sank as the ball sailed over him towards the back post. Surely it was going out of play. But

Joshua didn't give up on it. He dived desperately to head the ball across, and Florian swivelled to drill a low shot across the keeper. He looked up just in time to see it thump off the post and into the net, just like his strike against Scotland.

Goooooooooooooooooooooooooaaaaaaaaaaaaaaaaaaa aaaaaaalllllllllllllllllllllllllllllll!

Florian to the rescue! He ran to the fans with his arms outstretched and his mouth wide open in shock. It was one of the loudest roars he had ever heard at a football stadium, and it felt like every fan had just released the tension of the last hour. That goal had kept Germany's Euro 2024 dream alive.

'I knew that was going in, the second it landed in front of you!' Toni said, putting his arm round Florian.

But there was still a game to win, and Florian kept attacking. Then Spain struck the hammer blow with a winning goal in the 119th minute. The crowd went silent. Florian put his hands on his knees.

There was nothing anyone could say in the dressing room after a heartbreaking finish like that. Florian just sat there. He didn't want to shower and change. If he took off his shirt and shorts, it would confirm that the tournament was over. He wasn't ready for that yet.

But he had no choice. There would be no fairytale finish for Florian at Euro 2024, but his goals against Scotland, Germany's first of the tournament, and Spain, their last of the tournament, would live on. Two goals in his first European Championships wasn't bad.

Spain went on to beat England in the final, but Florian had already started looking ahead to next season at Leverkusen. He would take a few weeks off, but then it was back to work.

CHAPTER TWENTY-FOUR

NEW EXPECTATIONS AND A TASTE OF ANFIELD

It felt different to be the defending German league champions. Leverkusen had been such a surprise for most of last season, but now everyone knew what to expect. There would be fewer chances to sneak up on teams, and they had a target on their backs, with Bayern Munich hungry to take the title back.

'We're going to be tested again this year,' Xabi told his players. 'It's never easy to hit the same high levels the season after winning the title, but we've got to try. I believe in you guys.'

After winning the German Super Cup on penalties to lift another trophy, Leverkusen had to work hard for every point. They weren't blowing teams away in the same way as last season, and a home loss to RB Leipzig showed they had lost some of their aura.

Florian hoped that the thrill of the Champions League would provide a spark. Leverkusen had qualified for the competition after winning the German league, and he wouldn't have to wait long to hear that famous anthem. He got goosebumps just thinking about it.

These big European matches were the games where legends were made. This was where Lionel Messi and Cristiano Ronaldo had scored some of their most famous goals – and where underdog teams had pulled off major upsets.

When the draw was made, Florian smiled. Leverkusen were guaranteed to face some of the biggest teams on earth, and the random computer matched the club with Liverpool, AC Milan, Inter Milan and Atlético Madrid, among others, for the first round.

Those would all be special nights, but the trip to face Liverpool at Anfield was the one that Florian circled in his mind. He couldn't wait to see what that atmosphere would be like.

'This is the dream,' he told Juliane. 'We're playing with the big boys now, so I've got to be at my best.'

Florian proved he was up to the challenge. In the first Champions League game against Dutch club Feyenoord, Florian made a flying start. Leverkusen won the ball in midfield, and he dribbled forward into wide open space. With the ball on his left foot, he still felt confident, and he arrowed a low shot into the bottom corner.

Goooooooooooooooooooooooaaaaaaaaaaaaaaaaaaaa aaaaaaalllllllllllllllllllllllllllll!

Later in the first half, Jeremie burst clear on the right, and Florian sprinted to get into the box. He waved his arms to get his teammate's attention, and Jeremie's cross landed right on Florian's foot for a first-time finish.

Goooooooooooooooooooooooaaaaaaaaaaaaaaaaaaaa aaaaaaalllllllllllllllllllllllllllll!

When the Leverkusen squad arrived in England to face Liverpool, Florian could feel the mix of excitement and nerves he always got before big games. Xabi had tried to prepare his players for the emotions of a European night at Anfield, but Florian was still blown away by the spine-tingling buzz inside the stadium.

'Have you ever seen anything like this?' he asked Jeremie as they walked back towards the tunnel after the warm-up.

Jeremie shook his head. 'It's incredible!' he replied. 'No wonder it's so hard to win here.'

The crowd got louder as kick-off approached, and Florian stopped to look around the stands. Xabi had told him stories about his unforgettable Champions League wins here, and how the Kop end of the stadium seemed to suck the ball into the net when Liverpool were on top.

Just before kick-off, the Liverpool fans stood to sing 'You'll Never Walk Alone', their famous song. It was one of the most amazing moments that Florian had ever been a part of, with so much passion and emotion.

Florian knew that Liverpool were off to a good start

under their new manager, Arne Slot, and they had great players like Mo Salah and Virgil van Dijk.

For forty-five minutes, Leverkusen held firm, and Jeremie even had a goal disallowed. But then the roar of Anfield encouraged the home team, and Liverpool dominated the second half, racing to a 4–0 win.

Trudging off the pitch that night, Florian was unhappy with the result. It wasn't a true reflection of what Leverkusen could do, and he knew he hadn't been playing at his best. At the same time, though, he was grateful for the chance to experience playing at this famous stadium. It had opened his eyes even more to the quality of the Premier League, and he would be back in Liverpool sooner than he could have possibly expected.

CHAPTER TWENTY-FIVE

LIVERPOOL'S NEW PLAYMAKER

Leverkusen finished the 2024–25 season in second place but a long way behind Bayern Munich, who won the title by thirteen points. It was still a good season, yet it seemed disappointing in the shadow of last year's heroics.

There was also a feeling in the air that this Leverkusen era was coming to an end. Xabi was being linked with a move to Real Madrid, Jeremie was a transfer target for a few different teams and Florian began to think more about his own future.

As he did with any big decisions in his life, Florian sat down with his parents and talked through the different paths he could take. He called Juliane and asked for her opinion, too.

Florian had played in the German league for five seasons, and the Leverkusen journey had been amazing, with so many twists and turns. The club had shown so much faith in him, and he was proud to have repaid that faith with last season's heroics.

But this felt like the right moment to move on. After some hard conversations, Leverkusen understood his decision. Though they would have loved him to stay, they would agree to a transfer if they got a fair price for Florian. However, that price was high. Leverkusen valued Florian at more than £100 million.

As that news spread, the phones were soon ringing. Bayern Munich wanted to be at the front of the queue to sign Florian after watching his breakthrough over the last few years. If he was going to stay in Germany, Bayern Munich was an obvious choice.

But Florian was open to moving to other leagues,

and Liverpool made the strongest impression. They were already planning to sign Jeremie, and they saw Florian as the ideal playmaker to add to their attack.

He still had great memories of Anfield – not the result, but the magnetic atmosphere and the passion of the fans. He could really see himself wearing the red Liverpool shirt and playing in England.

Transfer offers went back and forth between Leverkusen and Liverpool, and Florian could only wait for updates. This was the hardest part. He couldn't think about the rest of his summer until he knew what was happening.

'As soon as there's any news, we'll know about it,' his dad reminded him. 'Until then, there's nothing we can do.'

Florian sat at his kitchen table with his phone in front of him, trying not to get swept up in the rumours and reports on social media. Eventually, he went to get some water. As he opened the cupboard to choose a glass, he heard his phone buzzing.

He hurried over. It was his dad.

'Flo, the deal is done!' Hans-Joachim explained. 'You're going to Liverpool.'

Florian froze. His head was spinning, and he had to sit down again to let it sink in. 'That's amazing,' he said. 'Wow, this is really happening!'

After that, everything moved quickly – the packing, the flight to England, the tour of Anfield and the training ground. Before he could blink, he was being introduced at a press conference, holding a Liverpool shirt with WIRTZ 7 on the back.

'I want to win everything every year,' he told reporters. 'Last season, Liverpool won the Premier League so my goal is for sure to win it again and also to go further in the Champions League. I'm really ambitious, and I'm really excited to have a new adventure in front of me.'

When Florian joined the Liverpool squad for their summer tour of Asia, he was determined to make a good first impression. Facing Yokohama FM, he was thrilled to be in the starting eleven, and it would be his first chance to link up with Mo, Cody Gakpo, Dominik Szoboszlai and the rest of Liverpool's attacking stars.

Florian's big moment came in the second half as Liverpool turned on the style. Mo slipped a pass through to him, and Florian made no mistake, slotting the ball past the keeper.

Gooooooooooooooooooooooooaaaaaaaaaaaaaaaaaaa aaaaaaalllllllllllllllllllllllllllll!

'Well, that didn't take you long!' Mo said, high-fiving him.

Florian grinned. It was nice to get his first goal and start building a connection with his teammates. During training sessions, Florian was getting a better understanding of how Coach Slot wanted his team to play, but he knew that real games would be the proper test.

Before he could get his first taste of Premier League action, he was on his way to London for the Community Shield at Wembley against Crystal Palace. He got off to a good start, setting up fellow new signing Hugo Ekitike for Liverpool's first goal. Celebrating with Hugo and Jeremie in front of the fans, he couldn't have been happier.

But the first game of the Premier League season

was the date that Florian was especially excited about. He wanted to experience Anfield as a Liverpool player, and he hoped the fans' passion would bring out the best in him.

That was the plan, at least.

CHAPTER TWENTY-SIX

GROWING PAINS IN THE PREMIER LEAGUE

Florian sighed as he trudged slowly off the pitch. Liverpool's season was spinning off track after a solid start, and he knew it had been another disappointing performance – for the team and for him personally.

His shoulders had slumped when he saw that Coach Slot was subbing him off, but he accepted that it hadn't been his best game. Despite all his success with Leverkusen and Germany, he could feel his confidence dipping. He was doing a lot of the same things that had worked for him at Leverkusen, but maybe he was trying too hard now.

This wasn't how he had pictured the first few

months at Liverpool, and it hurt. He was still trying to understand why he wasn't impacting games like he knew he could. He just hadn't expected the switch to Premier League football to be so challenging.

After winning the league last season, Liverpool had looked like the favourites again with their even stronger attack, but Florian, Mo, Hugo and Alexander Isak still needed time to gel.

There was extra attention on Florian, though. He was such a big signing – and the stats were concerning. In his first six matches in the Premier League, Florian had 0 goals and 0 assists.

He watched replays of the games and saw himself drifting around the pitch but not getting involved in the play enough. When he got chances to shoot, he was hesitating. In his best form, he would have already scored three or four goals. Florian paused the video and shook his head.

But Coach Slot wasn't panicking. 'Don't put extra pressure on yourself,' he explained, sensing the frustration and putting an arm around Florian's shoulders after training. 'This is all part of the process.

We still believe in you, and I'm still learning about how to put you in the best positions to shine.'

It was in moments like these that Florian really needed his support system – his parents, Juliane, the rest of the family and all his friends. Their messages kept him smiling and helped him ignore some negative comments online.

'These are just growing pains,' his dad said, echoing Coach Slot's advice. 'It can happen when you join a new club in a new country. The style of football is different, and it takes time to find your place in it.'

'It only takes a couple of good games to turn things around,' his mum added. 'Your luck is going to change.'

Of course, there seemed to be hundreds of opinions on why Florian was struggling. Most people accepted that it was still very early in his Liverpool career, but there were lots of comparisons made towards his Leverkusen form when he was more involved in the build-up play.

Slowly, though, Florian started to have a bigger impact. He came off the bench to help set up

Liverpool's equaliser against Manchester United, with a pass out wide that led to Cody's tap-in. The roar of the Anfield crowd made the hairs on Florian's arms stand up, and it felt amazing to contribute to the team. He had been at the club long enough to understand how important these games against United were for the fans.

'Great work, Flo!' Cody said, high-fiving him.

Then Florian had one of his best games in a Liverpool shirt against Eintracht Frankfurt in the Champions League, with two assists in a 5–1 win. The smile was back, and Florian could sense that he was getting closer to top form again.

'I know that I can do much, much more,' he told reporters after the game. 'I think the second half was really good, and from everyone else too.'

It was a reminder of how dangerous Florian could be in a free role, starting in a central position and then popping up on both wings. It helped him to make faster decisions, and he had the vision to link up with Liverpool's other attackers.

Florian still had plenty to prove – and so did

Liverpool after an inconsistent start to the season —
but he was feeling better about life in England. He
was still only twenty-two, and he was becoming more
comfortable with the speed and physicality of the
Premier League.

There had been some difficult moments over the
last few months, but now Florian couldn't wait for the
next game.

CHAPTER TWENTY-SEVEN

EYES ON THE BIGGEST PRIZES

Sometimes, there was so much attention on the next game and the next tournament that it was difficult to step back and see the bigger picture. Florian was still in the early stages of his career, and he might not reach his prime until he was twenty-seven or twenty-eight. In a way, he was ahead of schedule.

When he spoke to his friends back in Pulheim, they were quick to remind him how lucky he was to be playing football every day as his job.

'Flo, you've got a Premier League game on Saturday, then a Champions League game on Tuesday,' Christoph said. 'That's the dream! Just think of me sitting at a desk all day!'

Ever since winning tournaments with the Cologne academy, Florian loved chasing trophies. At Liverpool, there was the Premier League, Champions League and FA Cup to focus on, and he knew his role would keep growing with so many games on the fixture list.

The other big target was the 2026 World Cup with Germany. Euro 2024 had been an amazing ride, but they had lost in the quarterfinals. Since then, they had been on a good run in the UEFA Nations League, with Florian among the goalscorers. If the younger players in the team could build on those experiences, they would be real contenders when the next World Cup kicked off in the USA, Canada and Mexico.

'We've got even better since Euro 2024,' Florian insisted when he debated the possible squad with his friends. 'Just wait and see.'

He had been named the German Footballer of the Year in August 2025, and that was another massive honour, especially when he got a message from Toni, who had won the award in 2024.

'I can't think of a more worthy successor than you,'

Toni told him. 'I can't wait to see what you do next.'

Florian sat in his hotel room before Liverpool's latest Premier League match, and smiled as he looked back through photos on his phone.

There was one of his Under 17s Cologne team, and another of the Germany Under 21s team from Euro 2021. Then there was one of him and Jeremie at the German league title party, and another with Xabi. He also had photos with his family, all the way back to their camping trips and his early football days.

The last photos were with his Liverpool teammates. Mo and Virgil, Jeremie and Cody. Florian had never backed down from a challenge, especially on the football pitch, and proving himself in the Premier League was just the latest battle.

Florian put his phone away and got changed for the team meeting that was starting in fifteen minutes. There were big games ahead for club and country, and both Liverpool and Germany would be counting on him.

'Bring it on!' he said to himself, heading for the door.

Read on for a sneak preview of

another brilliant football story by

Matt and Tom Oldfield. . .

DEMBÉLÉ

Available now!

CHAPTER 1

SPRINTING TO GLORY

31 May 2025, Champions League Final,
Allianz Arena, Munich, Germany

Ousmane Dembélé was grinning as he walked into
the team meeting room. You would have never
known that he was about to play in the Champions
League final against Inter Milan. But that was just
Ousmane's style.

It didn't mean he was calm on the inside, though.
This was a huge moment for Paris St. Germain – or
PSG, for short – and he knew how long the club had
been waiting to get their hands on the Champions
League trophy. There had been some heartbreaking

European nights over the last ten years, and a few of the current squad had been there and had experienced those horror moments.

Of course, lifting this trophy would change all that. Ousmane had heard the talk on TV throughout the season. The media liked to say that PSG had reached another level since Lionel Messi, Neymar and Kylian Mbappé had all left – or that it was now a team of stars, not a collection of superstars – but Ousmane didn't like to think that way.

It *was* a new era, though. He could admit that. PSG had different players and a different style, with manager Luis Enrique in just his second year at the club.

PSG had already won the French league and cup double earlier in the month, so the season was just missing one last highlight to seal an unforgettable Treble.

'We've still got unfinished business.' That was the message in every meeting, and all the players knew that winning the Champions League would make them heroes for life in Paris.

When Coach Enrique had finished going over the game plan, Ousmane thought about the team's run of results to reach this final. He would never forget the feeling of scoring against Liverpool at Anfield, or setting up a key goal against Aston Villa.

It meant even more to Ousmane because he had grown up near Paris. Back then, he was a kid scrambling to get PSG tickets with his friends. Now he was a first-team star, and it was his shirt that thousands of fans would be wearing in the crowd. A lot had changed over the years.

Before falling asleep the night before, Ousmane thought about the experienced Inter team that stood in their way. The Italian club had fought hard to get this far, but he still felt good about PSG's chances with their match-winning talent all over the pitch:

Gianluigi Donnarumma, the giant goalie
Achraf Hakimi and Nuno Mendes, the
flying full-backs
Marquinhos, captain and centre-back colossus
Vitinha, the midfield magician

Khvicha Kvaratskhelia (Kvara) and Désiré Doué,
the wing wizards
And Ousmane himself, of course

Ever since he could dribble a ball, Ousmane had
been known for his attacking play. There were long
highlight videos packed with his mazy dribbles and
spectacular goals. But Coach Enrique had an extra job
for Ousmane in the final – and, for this, he wouldn't
have the ball at his feet.

'It's a simple plan really,' Coach Enrique explained.
'We're not giving Inter any time to get comfortable.
They like to play the ball around at the back from goal
kicks, so I want you leading the press from the edge
of the box as soon as they touch the ball.'

The coaches showed a few clips on the big screen.
Ousmane watched closely as Inter goalkeeper Yann
Sommer tapped a short pass to one of his defenders
inside the box.

'As soon as the ball is kicked, give us full-speed
pressing,' Coach Enrique said. 'Sprint until they panic.'
Ousmane nodded. He understood the job.

'There's no one faster than Dembouz!' Achraf
called out, using Ousmane's childhood nickname.

But it would take some practice to get it right.

'Wait, wait, go!' the coaches shouted as they
worked on the drill in training. 'Sprint! That's it,
Ousmane.'

Those instructions were still running through
Ousmane's head as he put on his Number 10 shirt and
walked out into the tunnel at Allianz Arena. These
minutes always seemed to go by so slowly! It was like
being back at school and waiting to go out for the
lunchtime football match.

The roar of the crowd told him that it was finally
showtime. The teammates in front of him were slowly
moving forward, and he followed them, looking ahead
to the glimpses of a green pitch. The atmosphere took
his breath away. He had played at the World Cup and
the European Championships, but this was up there
with the biggest nights of his career so far.

Ousmane didn't have to wait long to be part of the
action. On the first Inter goal kick, he stood on the
white line that marked the edge of the penalty area

and crouched into a sprinting position, like an athlete in the Olympic 100 metres final. An Inter defender looked at him in surprise, unsure what was happening.

As soon as Sommer played the usual short pass, Ousmane flew into the box like he was launched from a cannon. With four lightning steps, he was closing in on the ball – and Inter panicked, kicking the ball aimlessly up the pitch.

'Yes, Ousmane! Perfect!' the coaches yelled, giving him a thumbs up.

The rest of the first half was like a dream. Achraf made it 1–0 to finish off a quick team move, before Kvara floated a pass up the line to set Ousmane free on the left wing. The Inter defenders backed off, so Ousmane dribbled on. He curled a cross to Désiré, whose shot whistled into the net with the help of a deflection.

'Yeeeessssss!' Ousmane screamed, punching the air in delight. He ran over to celebrate with Désiré.

Inter didn't know what to do. Ousmane was soon back in position on the edge of the box. Again, he sprinted at full speed towards the Inter keeper and defenders, forcing a rushed pass. Another time, he almost blocked the clearance.

Behind him, he heard Vitinha and Kvara clapping his effort.

'Great work, Dembouz!' Vitinha shouted.

But Ousmane was still at his best when he was attacking. In the second half, PSG created more chances. Vitinha burst forward and slipped a pass to Ousmane. Without even glancing up, he knew what Vitinha was thinking. Ousmane fooled two Inter defenders with a genius back-heel into Vitinha's path for a killer one-two, leading to another beautiful goal for Doué. 3–0. It felt like the knockout blow.

Ten minutes later, Ousmane dropped deeper to get on the ball and spotted Kvara racing ahead of his marker. No one was tracking the run. Ousmane's pass was perfectly placed, and Kvara smashed a shot into the net. 4–0.

Now even the PSG subs were running to the corner flag to celebrate. The party had begun.

'What a pass!' Kvara shouted, hugging Ousmane and lifting him off the ground.

Ousmane smiled and encouraged his teammates to keep attacking. 'We want five!' he called to Vitinha when PSG won another corner.

Substitute Senny Mayulu smashed in a fifth goal just before full-time, and PSG's 5–0 victory became the biggest ever win in a Champions League final. Ousmane wasn't thinking about the history books, though. He wanted to get his hands on the trophy, which soon appeared with red and blue ribbons on the handles. 'I love this team!' he yelled as the size of their achievement sunk in.

Ousmane walked up behind Coach Enrique to get his medal. Then he huddled with his teammates on the podium while Marquinhos appeared with the trophy.

'Whoooooooooaaaaaaaa… Hurraaaaaaaaay!' they all screamed.

Campeones, Campeones, Olé! Olé! Olé!

Ousmane had played in enough big games to know what this night meant. Even the greatest teams rarely saved their best football for the biggest games, but that was exactly what Ousmane and PSG had done.

As Ousmane waved to his family and friends in the crowd, his smile widened. They deserved to be wearing this winner's medal too, and he knew that he would never have reached this moment without them.

Bayer Leverkusen

🏆 Bundesliga (German League): 2023–24

🏆 DFB-Pokal (German Cup): 2023–24

🏆 DFL-Supercup (German Super Cup): 2024

Germany U21

🏆 UEFA European Under-21 Championship: 2021

Individual

🏆 UEFA Europa League Young Player of the Season: 2022–23, 2023–24

🏆 UEFA Europa League Team of the Season: 2023–24

🏆 German Footballer of the Year: 2025

🏆 Bundesliga Player of the Season: 2023–24

WIRTZ

7 THE FACTS

NAME: Florian Richard Wirtz

DATE OF BIRTH: 3 May 2003

PLACE OF BIRTH: Pulheim, Germany

Age: 22

NATIONALITY: German

CURRENT CLUB: Liverpool

POSITION: CAM

THE STATS

Height (cm):	176
Club appearances:	211
Club goals:	57
Club trophies:	2
International appearances:	41
International goals:	10
International trophies:	1
BALLON D'ORS:	0

★ ★ ★ **HERO RATING: 88** ★ ★ ★

GREATEST MOMENTS

Florian's rapid rise was already drawing attention, but he really announced himself with a brilliant strike against Bayern Munich. It would have been easy to rush his chance, but he fooled a defender by cutting inside, then bent a shot past Manuel Neuer for a goal he would never forget. At 17 years and 34 days, Florian was now the German league's youngest ever scorer.

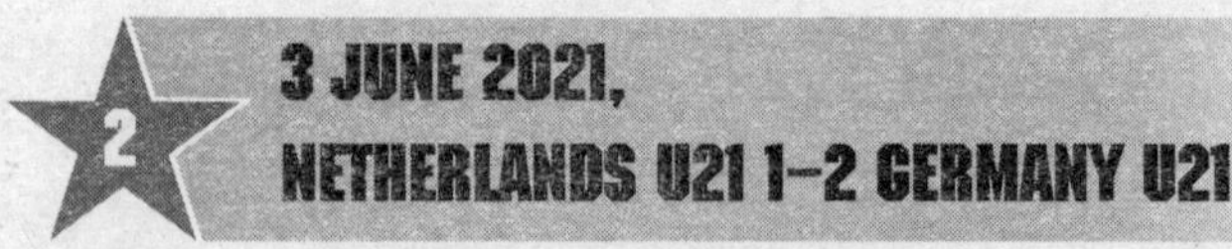

It was going to take something special for the German Under 21s team to get through this European Championships semifinal, and Florian delivered with a two-goal performance that left his teammates speechless. He reacted fastest in the box to put the Germans ahead, then doubled the lead with a low shot that beat the keeper's dive. Pressure? What pressure?

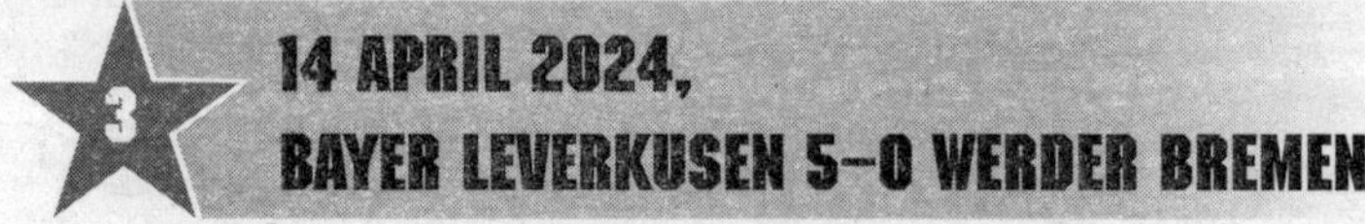

This was the day that Leverkusen clinched the German title for the first time, and Florian got the party started with a special hat-trick. His first was a rocket from outside the box, followed by two more clinical strikes. The win put the finishing touches on an unbeaten league season for Leverkusen, and the fans were soon celebrating on the pitch.

14 JUNE 2024,
GERMANY 5–1 SCOTLAND

As the Euro 2024 host nation, Germany played in the opening game of the tournament, and Florian made the perfect start, sweeping a shot into the net after just ten minutes. He was buried in hugs from his teammates as the crowd roared so loudly it felt like the whole country was packed inside the stadium. What a feeling!

22 OCTOBER 2025,
EINTRACHT FRANKFURT 1–5 LIVERPOOL

Florian was still looking for his first goal or assist as he returned to Germany to face Frankfurt in the Champions League. His early struggles, combined with a massive transfer fee, had raised doubts about whether he was a good fit for this team, but Florian responded in style in this game. With two assists in a runaway win, he reminded everyone why he was so highly rated.

TEST YOUR KNOWLEDGE

QUESTIONS

1. How old was Florian when he joined his first club, SV Grün-Weiß Brauweiler?

2. Where did Florian and his friends find their secret pitch?

3. Coach Heck managed Florian in which age group at the Cologne academy?

4. True or false: Florian made his Cologne debut against Borussia Dortmund.

5. Against which country did Florian score a quick-fire double in the Under 21 European Championships semifinal in 2021?

6. Why did Florian miss Leverkusen's Europa League game against Slavia Prague?

7. True or false: Florian's sister Juliane played for the Leverkusen women's team.

8. How long did it take Florian to score the first goal in Germany's friendly against France in March?

9. Who was Florian's manager when Leverkusen won the German league and cup double in the 2023–24 season?

10. How many goals did Florian score for Germany at Euro 2024?

11. What shirt number did Florian choose when he joined Liverpool?

1. Six years old 2. At school 3. Under-17s 4. False – it was against Werder Bremen 5. Netherlands 6. He had a school exam! 7. True! 8. Just seven seconds! 9. Xabi Alonso 10. Two 11. Number 7

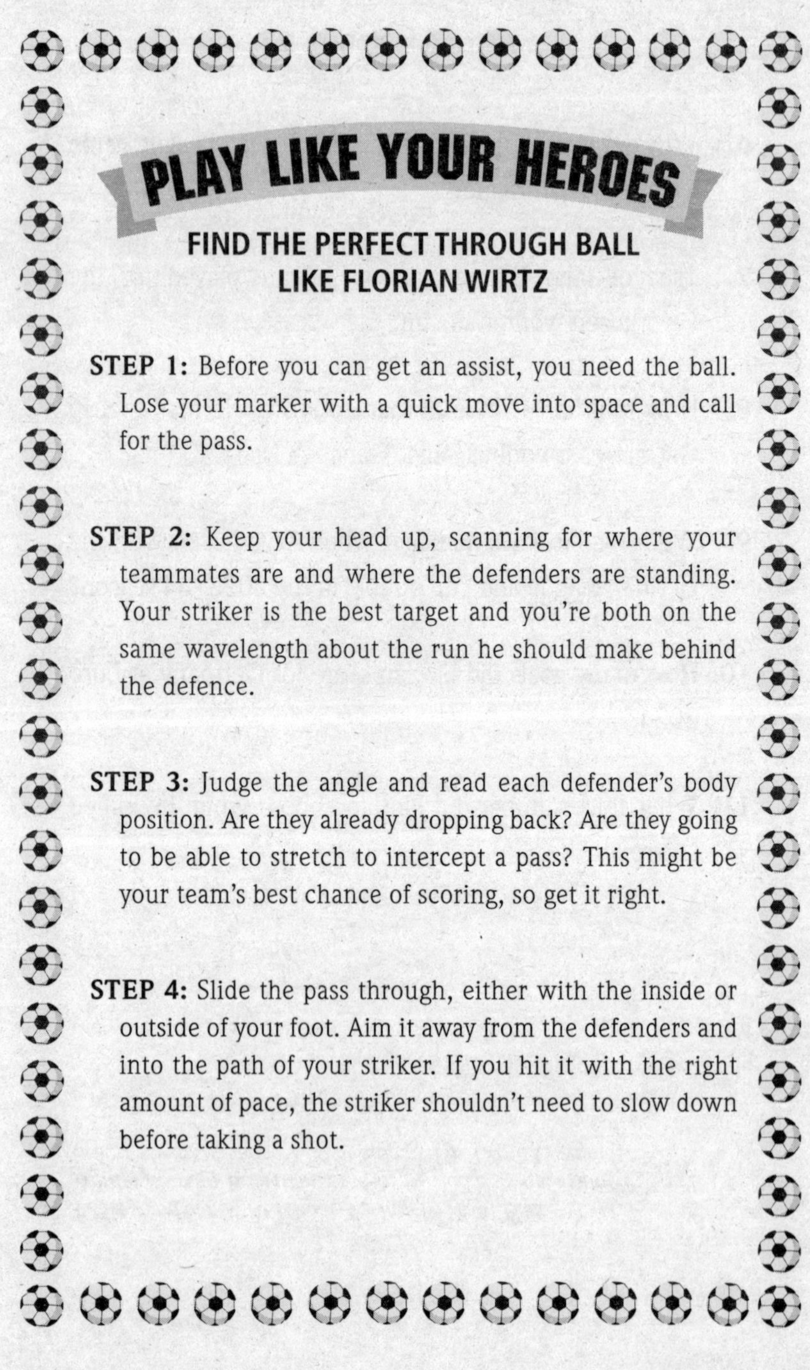

PLAY LIKE YOUR HEROES

FIND THE PERFECT THROUGH BALL
LIKE FLORIAN WIRTZ

STEP 1: Before you can get an assist, you need the ball. Lose your marker with a quick move into space and call for the pass.

STEP 2: Keep your head up, scanning for where your teammates are and where the defenders are standing. Your striker is the best target and you're both on the same wavelength about the run he should make behind the defence.

STEP 3: Judge the angle and read each defender's body position. Are they already dropping back? Are they going to be able to stretch to intercept a pass? This might be your team's best chance of scoring, so get it right.

STEP 4: Slide the pass through, either with the inside or outside of your foot. Aim it away from the defenders and into the path of your striker. If you hit it with the right amount of pace, the striker shouldn't need to slow down before taking a shot.

STEP 5: Don't just stand there and admire the pass — okay, you can admire it for a second, but then get forward in case there's a rebound. Hopefully you're seconds away from an assist, but there's no such thing as a guaranteed goal.

Check out heroesfootball.com
for quizzes, games, and competitions!

Plus join the Ultimate Football Heroes
Fan Club to score exclusive content and
be the first to hear about
new books and events.
heroesfootball.com/subscribe/